LIVING SPACES

THE ART AND METHODS OF INTERIOR DESIGN

Jin Yang, Wang Jin, Chen Xi, and Huang Yan

Copyright © 2024 Jin Yang, Wang Jin, Chen Xi, and Huang Yan

ISBN: 978-0-6483896-4-4

All rights reserved. No part of this book may be reproduced, translated, excerpted, reprinted, or adapted in any form or by any means without the written permission of the copyright owner.

Published by Asian Culture Press in June 2024

Asian Culture Press
247 South Rd. Mile End,
Adelaide, South Australia
5031, Australia

Distributed in the United States of America

Image Copyright Information
All images in this book are created by Jin Yang, and his team, with all rights reserved.
1. Cover Design: © 2024 Wang Jin
2. Chapter 1 Images: © 2024 Jin Yang, and his team
3. Chapter 2 Images: © 2024 Jin Yang, and his team
4. Chapter 3 Images: © 2024 Jin Yang, and his team
5. Chapter 4 Images: © 2024 Jin Yang, and his team
6. Chapter 5 Images: © 2024 Jin Yang, and his team
7. Chapter 6 Images: © 2024 Jin Yang, and his team

Special Acknowledgements
This section is located at the book's conclusion, where the specific contributions of the participants are clearly outlined in a detailed table.

For permission to use any images from this book, please contact the Author: jingyang84@zjut.edu.cn
For information on reprints, adaptations, or other licensing inquiries, please contact the Publisher: info@asianculture.press

A catalogue record for this work is available from the National Library of Australia

FOREWORD

Indoor living spaces have become the primary area of residence for contemporary individuals. With the rising standards of living, there is an increased emphasis on the expression of a personalized lifestyle. This encompasses an array of individual choices, including decor style, spatial layout, color schemes, furniture arrangement, and more. Unlike other interior areas, living spaces are uniquely tailored to reflect the habits or preferences of a family or individual. This necessitates a deep comprehension of the living space clients by those entering the field of interior design. When it comes to living room interiors, the focus is on designing for humans, marrying the presence of people with their environment. As designers, we often assume the role of facilitators.

This book unfolds over six chapters. The first four chapters concentrate on design principles. Beginning with a basic understanding of residential spaces, it progressively escorts the reader into the realm of design. You will be introduced to design philosophy and methodologies, discover the seamless fusion of form and functionality within spaces, and delve into the intrinsic traits and design ideologies of various spatial genres. The fifth and sixth chapters pivot to the strategies and techniques of interior design, as well as the detailed design and execution stages. These sections aim to impart a holistic understanding of the journey from conceptualization to the realization of design.

Moreover, the insights in this book are culled from the author's pedagogical and case study experiences at Zhejiang University of Technology in China. The case visuals presented to the reader are the culmination of educational and field practice. Consequently, this text also serves as a reflection on a decade's worth of practical engagement.

Additionally, this publication underscores the value of sharing hands-on experience. It intertwines the author's project-based wisdom with fundamental theories, facilitating a clearer comprehension and application of the imparted knowledge. Regardless of whether you're a professional in home interior design, a hobbyist of such aesthetics, or simply a homeowner yearning for an enhanced quality of life, this book promises to be a treasured guide, supporting you in crafting the home of your aspirations.

Jinyang, May 2024

Contents

Part 1

Cognitive Living Space Design
1. The Heart of Living Room Design — 2
2. The Transformation of Interior Spaces — 4
3. Feng Shui Fundamentals in Living Room Decor — 9
4. Future Trends in Living Room Interior Design — 12

Part 2

Strategies and Techniques in Living Room Interior Design
1. Integrating Artistry and Innovation in Living Room Decor — 16
2. Interior Design Concepts and Techniques — 17
3. Essentials of Living Room Layout — 19
4. Contrasting Yet Complementary: Living Room and Architectural Design — 23

Part 3

The Structure and Purpose of Living Room Interiors
1. Variety and Boundaries of Living Room Spatial Designs — 36
2. Spatial Function and Layout of the Living Room Interior — 40

Part 4

Types of Styles for Living Room Interiors
1. Overview of styles of living room interiors — 48
2. Chinese style — 48
3. New Chinese Style — 54
4. Japanese style — 57
5. European style — 61
6. American Style — 68
7. The Southeast Asian Style — 71
8. Modernist Style — 73
9. Industrial Retro Style — 76
10. Eclectic Mix and Match Style — 80

Part 5

Program for Living Spaces Design
1. Overall Process of Living Spaces Design — 84
2. Graphic Presentation in Living Spaces Design — 85

Part 6

Implementation and Construction Procedures of Living Spaces Design
1. Implementation Process of Interior Design in Living Spaces Design — 88
2. Construction of Living Spaces Design — 93

Cognitive Living Space Design

1. The Heart of Living Room Design
2. The Transformation of Interior Spaces
3. Feng Shui Fundamentals in Living Room Decor
4. Future Trends in Living Room Interior Design

Chapter 1: Cognitive living space design

Fig 1.1 Interior design coordinates the surrounding environment and the built environment to meet the material and spiritual needs of the occupants

1.1 The Heart of Living Room Design

Living spaces are architecturally designed responses to our basic human needs. Their importance in our lives is deeply entwined with the physical and emotional benefits they provide, driving their design and continual transformation.

Understanding Residential Spaces

We spend a significant chunk of our lives indoors, a setting where our cognition, productivity, quality of life, emotions, and aesthetic appreciation intersect. Ancient Roman architect Vitruvius famously stated that "*every room should be useful, sturdy, and beautiful,*" encapsulating the functional and emotional requirements of residential spaces.

Interior design roots itself in the practicality of a building, taking its surroundings, intended users, construction norms, and local environmental, aesthetic, and cultural influences into account. By blending scientific and technological strategies with architectural and design principles, interior design shapes spaces and their contents to meet functional demands, fulfill material and spiritual needs, and appeal to aesthetic preferences.

At the heart of every home are its living spaces. Leveraging interior design fundamentals, we delve into residents' specific needs, marrying modern innovations like advanced materials and home automation with timeless cultural values and various artistic expressions. This fusion fosters an environment that supports studying, living, working, resting, and playing—ultimately enhancing the home's soul and quality of life.

Core Tenets of Residential Space Design

Echoing the "*Bauhaus Manifesto*" by German architect Gropius, design should put people first—a philosophy at the heart of residential space design. Its primary goal is to fulfill the inhabitants' needs, merging architecture, interior, and landscape design within a theoretical framework. As Holly Joki noted, true design transcends mere decoration, weaving together social, economic, technical, artistic, and physiological threads for a targeted purpose. The challenge for designers is to blend these facets smoothly, creating spaces that are both beautiful and deeply meaningful.

Residential space design relies on several guiding principles:

Safety and Ecological Harmony

walls, and ceilings. Choosing durable materials and ensuring solid construction bonds is the first step to reinforcing safety.

Green Design: Sustainable design is crucial. Selecting materials that adhere to national safety standards prevents the emission of harmful substances like formaldehyde, ammonia, radon, and benzene, paving the way for a healthier, eco-friendly home.

Functional Safety: Practical safety considerations are also paramount. This encompasses good indoor ventilation and lighting, fire safety measures, and tailored strategies to protect vulnerable groups like children and the elderly from household hazards.By weaving together these principles, designers can craft living rooms that captivate and comfort, serving as functional, safe, and sustainable havens for all who dwell within.

The golden rule of blending functionality with aesthetics

In the realm of interior design, it's crucial to avoid designs that are purely for show or overly extravagant. It's not uncommon for budding designers to add too many decorative elements or unnecessary features to living room designs, either to flex their creative muscles or to fulfill extravagant client wishes, leading to resource wastage and eventual design burnout. It's key to remember that the living room, a space for personal or family daily activities, has different needs compared to public spaces.

Fig 1.2 Principle of integration of function and decoration: material and shape are all elements that enhance the decorative sense of furniture

In designing a living room, striking a balance between its functional and aesthetic aspects is vital, without tipping the scales too much in either direction. Designers should strive to craft spaces that support daily life activities—be it lounging, working, studying, or entertaining—comfortably. Utilizing design elements, motifs, and artistic expressions, designers can capture and express the room's emotional core. Through thoughtful visual touches and the crafted ambiance, the design should meet the inhabitants' psychological and aesthetic requirements, making the living room a true haven.

Principle of applicability

As the ancient text "*Kaogong Ji*" states, "*Heaven has its timing, earth possesses its essence, materials hold their beauty, and craftsmanship reveals skill. When these four elements are harmoniously combined, excellence emerges.*" This underscores the importance of functionality in both architectural structures and furnishings. Interior design is not merely about the lavish use of premium materials; rather, each material and technique should serve a specific purpose in the space. Instead of chasing high renovation costs, a proficient designer should aim to "*use materials to their fullest and employ craftsmanship wisely,*" fulfilling user needs within the most economical means.

Fig 1.3 Principle of Practicality: Satisfying the Living Habits, Aesthetics, and Economic Conditions of Occupants

This approach resonates with the minimalist design philosophy prevalent in Japan and other countries. As a designer, it's essential to consider not only the occupants' needs but also their social and economic capacities. Design should be customized to the owners' actual circumstances and living standards, striving for a harmonious balance between practicality and artistic aesthetics. Elevating design standards indiscriminately, resulting in excessive spending, does not equate to good design. Rather, exceptional design involves employing effective and precise design techniques and methods to achieve superior functionality and aesthetic appeal within the same budget constraints.

1.2 The Transformation of Interior Spaces

Over the years, the design of room interiors has evolved into a specialized niche within the vast world of interior design. Historically linked with architectural design, interior design reflects the progression of a region, nation, or culture. The way living spaces are designed is a key indicator of the inhabitants' lifestyle, activities, and cultural legacy. Before getting into the nuts and bolts of living room design, it's crucial to grasp the historical context of human indoor environments, which closely tracks with the development of architecture through the ages.

The Evolution and Traits of International Architectural Interiors

The Ancient Egyptian Era

Fig 1.4 Ancient Egyptian Decorative Style

Situated in North Africa's Nile Valley, ancient Egypt is hailed as one of humanity's birthplaces of civilization. Its origins trace back approximately 7,450 years to the Fayoum region (around 5450 BC), with its era concluding with the Arab Empire's Islamicization in 639 AD. Ancient Egypt's rich cultural tapestry, highlighted by its influential hieroglyphics, played a critical role in shaping the Phoenician alphabet, which subsequently birthed the Greek alphabet. Egyptians were architectural trailblazers, erecting some of the earliest and most impressive structures known, alongside intricate interior designs. They introduced the world's initial solar calendar, pioneered advancements in geometry and surveying, and utilized orthographic projection in architectural drawings—plans, elevations, and sections—with remarkable accuracy.

The monumental legacy of ancient Egypt, featuring the iconic pyramids and the Temple of Amun at Karnak, stands testament to their architectural and interior design prowess. Inside, they exhibited exquisite craftsmanship, converting stone and wood into practical yet decorative items like tools, furniture, utensils, and artistic pieces, thereby elevating their interior aesthetics. Their walls were adorned with shallow relief carvings and painted frescoes that captured ritualistic scenes, hunting expeditions, and everyday life, mirroring their deep appreciation for nature's beauty. The decorative ethos of ancient Egypt was marked by its simplicity, majesty, and a preference for stonework. The Egyptian columnar style remains a hallmark of their architectural genius, encapsulating the quintessence of their interior decorating skills.

Ancient Greek Period: Architectural Legacy

The ancient Greeks inherited their architectural prowess from the Mycenaean civilization. Initially starting with timber for structural support, by the Greek Primitive Republic era (409 B.C.), they had transitioned to high-grade stone for their buildings. The hallmark of ancient Greek architecture is the prevalent use of stone, especially in however, due to stone's limited ability to handle lateral loads, load-bearing beams and slabs rarely exceeded 3 meters. The remarkable vertical load-bearing quality of stone established columns as the main structural element, often configured into exterior colonnades, interior stacking, and pairs with beams, slabs, and robust load-bearing walls. Greek architects utilized three iconic column styles: Doric, Ionic, and Corinthian.

The rigidity of thick load-bearing walls generally eliminated the possibility of window openings without the innovation of concrete, giving rise to a signature Greek interior characterized by prolific columns and scant windows, leading to a subdued and austere interior ambiance. The use of stone imparts a sense of coolness and majesty, with walls typically bare and free from bright colors. Greek architecture shines in its sculptural finesse with its columns, architectural carvings, and thematic reliefs, including round carvings, high and shallow reliefs, which elevate the structures to sculptural masterpieces. The two-sloped roofs of these buildings often showcased decorative pediments, adding to the buildings' sculptural appeal.

Greek architecture is, in essence, a collection of stone sculptures, from the intricately designed Ionic and Corinthian capitals replete with motifs from nature, to the elaborate mythological reliefs adorning temple fronts. Such intricate carvings demonstrate the Greeks' advanced artistic sensibilities and their deep admiration for the aesthetics of the human form and the harmony of proportions. The Greek celebration of human body proportions, whether in sculpture or architecture, is viewed as a paragon of perfection.

Ancient Rome: Architectural Innovations

Ancient Roman architecture blossomed from the seeds planted by Greek and Etruscan influences on the Italian Peninsula. Drawing from these roots, the Romans revolutionized architectural forms, techniques, and aesthetics, not only amplifying the grandeur of Greek art through advanced technical prowess but also translating the harmonious, perfect, and sublime essence of Greek architecture into a more worldly context. This adaptation enriched Roman architecture with fresh aesthetic pursuits and distinctive formal traits.

Distinctive features of ancient Roman architecture include its sturdy masonry walls, semicircular arches, elaborate doorframes, and the strategic use of cross-vaulted structures. A standout innovation was the Roman adoption of concrete to construct vaulted and domed structures, a technique not seen in ancient Greek architecture. The Romans also incorporated Greek column styles—Doric, Corinthian, and Ionic—often blending them with Tuscan elements. When these columns were paired with arches, they became a signature element of Roman architectural design, marking a significant departure from their Greek predecessors.

Fig 1.5 Ancient Roman Colosseum

Medieval Europe: An Architectural Journey

The Middle Ages, stretching from the fall of the Western Roman Empire in 476 A.D. to the demise of the Eastern Roman Empire in 1453 A.D., saw Europe navigating through times of decentralized power, with the Church playing a pivotal role in shaping Western culture and

This era birthed two significant architectural movements: Byzantine and Gothic.

Byzantine Style

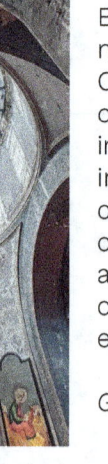

Byzantium, initially a Greek fortress, ascended as the capital of the Eastern Roman Empire in 395 A.D. following the empire's division. This marked the beginning of what would be known as the Byzantine Empire. Characterized by its extensive use of vaulted roofs and commanding central domes, Byzantine architecture paved the way for a structural innovation: domes supported by autonomous square columns, ushering in a new era of centralized building designs. Unlike traditional Greek columns, Byzantine columns stand out with their inverted square conical capitals, adorned with motifs of the natural world, incorporating Persian and Greek influences. The style is celebrated for its vivid Eastern colors, central motifs, geometric adornments, and an atmosphere charged with emotion, painted in bright hues.

Fig 1.6 Sofia Church

Gothic Architecture

The Gothic style, originating in 11th-century France, reshaped European architecture between the 13th and 15th centuries. It symbolized a cultural renaissance, responding to the evolving European civilization. Gothic architecture is renowned for its domes, columns, towers, stained glass windows, vaults, and arches. A prime example of this style, the Cologne Cathedral dazzles with its intricate interior and extensive use of stained glass, predominantly featuring biblical scenes. This stained glass artwork floods the interior with color and light, creating an aura of sanctity and divinity.

This architectural style left a lasting impact on various art forms, including painting and sculpture, and even influenced furniture design and fashion trends. Inspired by the slender, towering structures of Gothic architecture, medieval European fashion embraced a *"narrow waist culture,"* setting the stage for modern Western fashion norms.

Unveiling the European Renaissance: A Catalyst for Modern Intellectual Freedoms

The Renaissance, a pivotal intellectual and cultural movement, originated in mid-14th century Italy and expanded across Western Europe, peaking in the 16th century. This era marked a profound transformation in science and the arts, signaling the shift from feudalism to capitalism, according to Marxist historians. Together with the Reformation and the Enlightenment, the Renaissance stands as one of the triad of movements that heralded modern intellectual freedoms in Western Europe.

Post the 13th century, a cadre of influential humanists and artists including Dante, Giotto, Leonardo da Vinci, Michelangelo, and Brunelleschi, emerged as champions of human potential. They fervently advocated for the exploration of the objective world, the development of human nature, self-expression, the enjoyment of life, and the appreciation of beauty. Drawing inspiration from the classical Italian and Byzantine cultures—the latter having succumbed to the Turks—they

Renaissance, a term synonymous with the revival of classical culture. By the 15th century, the ideals of the Renaissance had begun to influence the feudal rulers of central and northern Italy and the Holy See, culminating in Rome becoming the epicenter of the movement in the 16th century. The Renaissance's influence on architecture and interior design manifested in several significant ways:
1. Secular buildings became more diverse and sophisticated, catering to everyday life.
2. Architectural typologies and artistic forms saw substantial innovation.
3. Ancient Roman arches and advancements in dome construction technology adorned large structures.
4. Architects transcended their craft status to become versatile, influential figures.
5. Architectural theory flourished, producing numerous scholarly works.
6. The classical style was revived, with the columnar system reemerging as a fundamental architectural element.
7. Many architects became cultural pioneers, with their works marking historical milestones.

In the heart of the Renaissance, the grand villas of Rome stood as testaments to the revival of ancient Roman design principles, epitomized by the majestic Farnese residence. This architectural masterpiece boasts a square courtyard framed by colonnades rising across three levels. The arcades, supported by sturdy piers rather than delicate columns, enhance the structure's vertical prowess as the capitals themselves brace the eaves.The crown jewel of the residence, the Gades Hall, is an awe-inspiring space extending up two floors, with its windows and columns echoing the building's stately exterior. The classical allure of the villa is further amplified by the door frames, richly paneled wooden ceilings, and meticulously laid floors. Adorning the walls are small, round reliefs and vibrant tapestries, striking a balance between simplicity and elegance without tipping into over-embellishment.Diverse in their decor, other rooms are tailored to their designated roles, often graced with ceiling and wall paintings that breathe life into mythological scenes. Some walls present figures in three dimensions set within painted frames, creating an illusion of depth reminiscent of the frescoes in the ancient homes of Pompeii.This careful curation of interior elements not only serves their functional purposes but also weaves a tapestry of classical beauty, reviving the timeless charm of Roman architectural traditions.

Inside Islamic Worship: The Humble Beginnings

The interior spaces of Islamic buildings are steeped in history, and their defining elements date back to the very first Islamic place of worship—the Prophet Muhammad's home in Medina. This space was distinguished by a spacious courtyard with a simple yet central dwelling. A defining feature was the row of sturdy date palm trunk pillars that lined one side of the courtyard, supporting a pergola fashioned from the fronds of the same trees. This natural canopy offered a cool, shaded haven for worshippers to gather under the hot desert sun. The Prophet himself would lead prayers from the porch of this room, setting a precedent for the communal and unadorned nature of Islamic worship spaces. This original setting showcases the hallmarks of Islamic creating a welcoming space for spiritual congregation. It's a blueprint that has resonated through centuries, capturing a simplicity and reverence that still echoes in Islamic architecture today.

Evolution of Islamic Mosque Design

The design evolution of Islamic mosques is a fascinating narrative of spiritual devotion and architectural innovation. Beginning with the Kuba Mosque in Mecca, constructed by the Prophet Muhammad in merely four days, mosques have served as pillars of Islamic faith. The Kuba Mosque, often cited in the Qur'an as *"a mosque founded on piety from the first day,"* laid the foundational design for subsequent mosques.

A significant milestone in Islamic architecture was the construction of the Dome of the Rock Mosque in Jerusalem in 691 A.D. Its dome, adorned with the pioneering use of arabesque patterns, introduced the world to the beauty of repetitive decorative motifs on its upper surfaces, setting a precedent for future Islamic architectural endeavors.

By 847 A.D., the Great Mosque of Samarra in Iraq further expanded the architectural lexicon with its introduction of the minaret—a slender, towering structure serving not just as a beacon for the preacher or caller to summon the faithful to prayer, but also as a profound symbol of submission to God. The utilitarian aspect of the minaret's height, which aided sound transmission across distances, intertwined seamlessly with its spiritual symbolism. Together, domes and minarets have become quintessential elements of Islamic mosques, representing a blend of practicality and profound spiritual meaning.

The Blue Mosque in Istanbul, a masterpiece of Ottoman architecture designed by Mehmet Aga, a student of the famous architect Sinan, stands as a testament to the enduring allure of Islamic design. Named for its interior, resplendent with blue and white tiles, the mosque reflects the significance of blue—a color cherished by the Prophet Muhammad and deeply symbolic in Islamic culture. Constructed without the use of nails, this architectural marvel has withstood the test of time and natural disasters. Its 260 windows, over 20,000 blue tiles, lavish carpets, and intricate Arabic calligraphy continue to draw admirers from around the globe, embodying the rich legacy and evolving aesthetic of Islamic mosques.

Diversity in Chinese Interior Decoration

China, nestled in southeastern Asia, encompasses a vast and diverse landscape, bordered by the Pacific Ocean to the east and the Tibetan and Pamir Plateaus to the west. Its climate, predominantly influenced by monsoons, varies from subfreezing to temperate and subtropical zones, shaping a rich tapestry of architectural styles.

During the Neolithic era (circa 10,000-4,000 B.C.), Chinese architecture diverged based on regional climates. In the south, where humidity and warmth prevailed, dwellings focused on dryness, evolving from primitive nests to elevated wooden platforms, such as those seen in the 7,000-year-old Hemudu culture. In contrast, the dry, cold north favored geothermal heat retention, leading to the popularity of cave dwellings, mountain kilns, and sunken kilns.

As time advanced, southern architecture developed to include airy structures such as the long-ridged, short-eaved homes found in the Yunnan-Guizhou area. Simultaneously, in the middle and lower Yellow River Basin, central communal dwellings emerged, as seen at sites like Xi'an's Half-slope and Lintong Jiangzhai. Residential architecture shifted from underground caves and semi-subterranean structures to above-ground buildings with thatched roofs on mud-plastered wooden frames. Decorative art in living spaces is a fundamental human need, closely tied to our survival and development. Evidence from the Hemudu and Yangshao cultures in the Yellow River Basin indicates that our ancestors sought to enhance the rationality, comfort, and safety of their homes through careful design and decoration, fostering a harmonious relationship between nature and human habitation.

Over the centuries, wooden structures have become a hallmark of traditional Chinese architecture and interiors. These systems serve as enclosures, with beams and columns bearing loads, while arches and beams play both structural and decorative roles. Interior design emphasizes symmetry, incorporating ceiling panels, furnishings, and artwork. Spaces are divided by movable screens and fixed partitions, enhanced by semi-open shelves and strategic furniture placements that add depth and complexity. Vertical elements like carved beams, painted panels, and ceilings are adorned with intricate details. Influenced by Confucianism, Buddhism, and Taoism, Chinese interior decoration exhibits a scholarly aesthetic, featuring calligraphy, paintings, and porcelain to create a refined and subtle atmosphere. This tradition, rooted in Han culture, has evolved into a distinctive style known as China's *national traditional form*," enduring through centuries and still prevalent today.

Fig 1.7 Hemudu Site

Chinese architecture, deeply ingrained in an agricultural society, consistently champions the ideology of *man and nature as one*." This principle mirrors the teachings of Confucianism, Buddhism, and Taoism, each shaping architectural and interior design in distinct ways. Confucianism, with its focus on hierarchical order and ritual, inspires stable, mature, and subtly profound spatial arrangements, often symmetric and anchored by a central axis, as showcased in palaces. Taoism, which prizes natural harmony and individuality, nudges design toward personal expression and a profound bond with nature. Buddhism, aiming for self-discipline and enlightenment, influences the creation of simple, tranquil living spaces. These philosophical roots are visible in the layout and decorative aspects of buildings, offering a treasure trove of design inspiration for modern creators.

Fig 1.8 Shrine of Our Lady

1.3 Feng Shui Fundamentals in Living Room Decor

Feng Shui, a time-honored Chinese philosophy, revolves around the belief that the flow of wind (Feng) and water (Shui), along with various environmental elements, plays a critical role in shaping a family's fortune. This ancient wisdom extends beyond selecting homes or gravesites; it is pivotal in interior design, especially in crafting the perfect living room ambiance. At the heart of Feng Shui is the manipulation and

The mantra "*Form and potential coalesce to form qi, and the behavior of qi is contingent upon form,*" highlights Feng Shui's reliance on the surroundings. It's an art form that advocates for a seamless blend with the environment, striving for a "*unity of man and nature.*" This principle not just enriches our living spaces but echoes a deeper, timeless philosophy of living in balance and harmony with the natural world. Feng Shui, in essence, invites us to embrace nature's rhythm, transforming our homes into sanctuaries of peace, prosperity, and health.

The Modern Scientific Approach to Feng Shui in Interior Design

Feng Shui, once steeped in traditional Chinese divination and metaphysical concepts like yin and yang, has undergone a transformation in contemporary interior design. It now encompasses a more scientific and psychological approach, blending traditional Chinese psychology and natural science with design principles. This holistic discipline is grounded in the psychological responses of occupants, incorporating the "*Yi culture's*" notions of "*unity of man and nature*" and "*interconnectedness of all things.*" At its core, Feng Shui explores the psychological impact of the interaction between humans and their natural environment.

The environment speaks through "*spatial language*" and "*spatial behavior,*" such as openness versus enclosure, and privacy versus publicness, influencing individual activities and interpersonal interactions within the living room. A comfortable and vibrant living environment can foster positive attitudes, assist in emotional regulation, promote family harmony, and satisfy both physiological and psychological needs. In modern interior design, designers create an atmosphere of tranquility and auspicious comfort by carefully selecting materials, colors, lighting, layout, and decorations, all tailored to the occupants' needs and perceptions of indoor space.

As modern science progresses, Feng Shui, rooted in natural science principles and the living habits and behaviors of occupants, has emerged as a vital component of human living environments. "*Feng*" refers to air quality and circulation within the living space, and "*Shui*" relates to humidity and water resources, both critical for human survival. When harmoniously integrated with overall meteorological conditions and natural elements, these factors contribute to a safe, clean, and enduring living environment, supporting the sustainable survival and development of its inhabitants.

Feng Shui's alignment with human survival laws and environmental conservation concepts has been consistent throughout history. Modern architectural interior design, informed by a scientific understanding of Feng Shui, confirms that its principles are essential for creating favorable living conditions. For example, to prevent the infiltration of highly pathogenic corrosive gases from sewer backwash during high winds or drastic air pressure changes, functional spaces like kitchens and bathrooms are strategically located on the north side of residences, enhancing the healthy living environment.

Applying Cultural Feng Shui Principles

Principle of Organic System

orchestra where each element plays a crucial part in the symphony of space. The ancient text "*The Yellow Emperor's Classic of Mansions*" paints a holistic picture: envision the landscape as a living organism, where the terrain forms its physique, springs its lifeblood, and vegetation its lustrous locks. Structures are akin to clothing, and doorways, the ornaments that signify grace and prosperity. Feng Shui fosters the notion of "*unity of heaven and man,*" conceiving the environment as a human-centric, living tapestry that weaves together earthly and celestial elements.

In this interconnected web, each component plays a supporting role, transforming and interacting to maintain equilibrium. The interior space is the stage, with humans as the directors and the room's structural features as the cast, each performing its part yet working in concert to create a harmonious living area. Feng Shui's art lies in tuning these relationships, just as one would fine-tune an instrument, ensuring the space is not only aesthetically pleasing but also optimized for well-being and prosperity.

Fig 1.9 Every element of the interior interacts with each other and with each other

The Principle of Adapting to Local Conditions in Feng Shui

China's expansive geography and varied climates significantly shape the requirements and quality of human dwellings, resulting in diverse architectural and interior design styles across regions. Architectural forms and interior aesthetics are tailored to the objective conditions of the natural and social environment, including climate, soil, vegetation, economic development, political influences, and local customs. For example, in the humid southwest, elevated stilted houses are prevalent, providing upper levels for ventilation and moisture protection, while lower levels serve as storage or livestock areas. In the water-abundant Jiangnan region, homes often face both streets and rivers, featuring whitewashed walls for waterproofing. Architectural styles within the south differ markedly, with even starker contrasts between the north and south. Localized design considerations are crucial to accommodate these regional nuances.

Feng Shui, as a vital method for adapting to local conditions, integrates the micro-environment into the broader context, often favoring a north-facing orientation. The "*Historical Records - Book of Laws*" notes: "*The winds of Buzhou reside in the northwest in October, those of Guangmao in the north in November, the wind of the strip in the northeast in January, and the Mingshu wind in the east in February.*" Given China's topographical environment, which fosters a monsoon climate, south-facing houses are optimal for capturing abundant sunlight for warmth and daily activities. Statistics indicate that south-facing rooms in winter are 1-3 degrees Celsius warmer than their north-facing counterparts, effectively buffering the harshness of the north wind during colder months.

Fig 1.10 Adapting to the local environment by framing views through floor-to-ceiling windows

The Natural and Environmental Principles of Feng Shui

Feng Shui's core principle of natural environmental protection

Fig 1.11 Introducing plant landscaping in the interior to form a sense of natural animation in the space

energies, enabling all things to self-generate." In this philosophy, mountains are seen as the earth's bones, and water is revered as the lifeblood. An ideal living environment is one where mountains embrace water, a design that not only reflects ancient survival needs but also societal values.

In urban settings, incorporating natural elements into living spaces should honor the intrinsic beauty of the landscape. Different natural elements elicit unique visual and psychological reactions. Designers must deeply understand the residents' needs and the characteristics of natural elements, including their types, materials, forms, colors, and shapes. By scientifically and reasonably integrating greenery, materials, and ambient light, designers can fulfill residents' spatial experiences and needs, while also facilitating convenient living activities and preserving the natural aesthetic.

1.4 Future Trends in Living Room Interior Design

As science progresses and civilization advances, the integration of interior design with other disciplines is intensifying. With the rapid pace of urbanization, we're seeing a significant shift in human lifestyles. Interior design is now grappling with challenges like environmental pollution, aging populations, and food safety. In response, the architecture and interior design sectors are increasingly embracing innovative designs and technologies, using new materials and techniques to foster green, eco-friendly, and smart living environments aimed at creating a sustainable and healthy future.

Fig 1.12 Space capsule bedroom, space integrating technological elements and emerging materials into interior design

One emerging trend is intensive design, which responds to the growing need for efficient space utilization as natural resources dwindle and society evolves. This concept focuses on maximizing the use of each square foot while maintaining living quality. Modern solutions like "*apartment houses*," "*SOHO*," and "*micro homes*" reflect this shift towards accommodating new living needs and diverse lifestyles. Achieving a balance between space efficiency and resident comfort is key. This means utilizing innovative materials and technologies to ensure spaces are flexible and multifunctional—think adjustable furniture and movable walls to meet varying needs. Additionally, these spaces emphasize energy conservation and environmental protection to minimize both energy use and pollution in both construction and daily use.

Fig 1.13 Emerging Materials and Life Forming New Lifestyles and Aesthetic Trends

The shift towards intelligent design is a pivotal trend in modern living room interiors. With the rapid evolution of mobile communication and technology, many once-futuristic gadgets have seamlessly woven into our everyday existence. The concept of smart homes has evolved from mere "*home automation*" to sophisticated "*home networking*," and further to "*networked appliances*" and "*information appliances*." In this intelligent design approach, it's crucial to center on the residents' needs, enhancing their living experience with smart technologies such as adaptive lighting, smart thermostats, and advanced security systems. This integration aims to create a living space that is not only more convenient and comfortable but also secure.

Furthermore, smart home design plays a pivotal role in resource conservation, slashing energy consumption and waste. Consider intelligent lighting systems that dynamically respond to natural light or smart thermostats that tailor temperature settings to user habits and weather changes, all contributing to energy savings. Beyond functionality, smart home design also imbues interiors with a sleek, futuristic flair, elevating the living space's overall quality and aesthetic appeal.

Finally, delving into green design trends reveals a deeper commitment to eco-friendly living. Green housing is not just about adding more plants or decorative rooftop gardens. It's about forging a sustainable connection between humans and the environment through thoughtful residential building and design, optimizing resource use. Green design pushes the boundaries of traditional architecture and interior decorating. It aims to craft sustainable, economically sound homes that minimize waste and eliminate pollution by intelligently integrating internal and external systems. This approach includes using eco-friendly, biodegradable, and non-toxic materials to reduce reliance on synthetic substances; harnessing clean energy sources like sunlight for better energy efficiency; and thoughtfully designing outdoor spaces with vertical greening methods, such as trellises, to preserve and enhance the surrounding natural ecosystem and its stability.

Through green ecological design, individuals can enjoy a healthy and comfortable living space while benefiting the natural environment. Merging green design with smart, efficient strategies leads to living spaces that are not only more sustainable and energy-efficient but also comfortable and visually appealing. This harmonious blend paves the path to a brighter future for humanity.

Fig 1.14 Green into Life

Strategies and Techniques in Living Room Interior Design

1. Integrating Artistry and Innovation in Living Room Decor
2. Interior Design Concepts and Techniques
3. Essentials of Living Room Layout
4. Contrasting Yet Complementary: Living Room and Architectural Design

Chapter 2: Strategies and Techniques in Living Room Interior Design

2.1 Integrating Artistry and Innovation in Living Room Decor

Interior design, at its core, mirrors the broader design ethos: enhancing practicality through aesthetics. Art and science serve as the bedrock, driving innovation and creativity in living spaces. This synergy not only infuses the area with emotional and artistic charm but also guarantees the functionality of the living environment.

The design process involves distilling intricate external elements and sensations into coherent, artistic concepts, crafting environments that resonate with human emotions and behaviors. This approach seamlessly blends knowledge with emotion, culminating in a system that harmonizes artistic aesthetics with scientific principles

The Art of Design

Art provides a distinctive human lens on the world, weaving together emotion and imagination. It reinterprets reality through aesthetic endeavors that embody emotional ideals, creating a symbiosis of the aesthetic subject and object in the realm of imagination. Art specifically mirrors people's daily lives and their inner landscapes, stemming from the artist's holistic mental processes that include perception, emotion, ideals, and thoughts.

As a designer, it's essential to not only meet functional requirements but also to keenly observe external stimuli and human connections, designing spaces that infuse life with beauty, detail, and a revitalized experience of the original living environment. This approach ensures that design not only serves practical needs but also enriches our emotional and imaginative lives.

This Stuttgart loft's salon-style room bursts with a lively blend of contrasting hues, bold graphics, and expansive shapes. The area features large, vividly colored geometric carpets and artistic furniture like Mustache chairs, all complemented by decorative paintings that subtly elevate the decor. The living space showcases a dynamic array of the owner's global travels and art market finds, depicting a life steeped in rich experiences. Tolstoy described art as *"the attempt to express the highest and most profound emotions experienced by humans."* In this context, interior designers can focus on the "living object," merging literature, music, and visual arts to deeply probe and reflect the dwellers' life and emotions. This exploration is artistically conveyed in the design, which should not only focus on form but also incorporate bold, innovative techniques to enrich the ambiance.

Fig 2.1:Artistry of design

The Craft of Design

Science extends beyond "*a body of knowledge reflecting the nature and laws of phenomena through categories, theorems, and laws.*" It classifies social ideologies into natural sciences, social sciences, and thinking sciences, with philosophy and mathematics as overarching disciplines intersecting these fields. In design, the scientific method mirrors human thought processes, enabling rational outcomes through careful planning, observation, and purposeful experimentation.

The ground level is segmented into zones for welcoming guests, dining, and leisure, each mirroring distinct lifestyle functions. The upper level is exclusively for relaxation. This zoning promotes systematic organization of the home's interior, both globally and locally. It allows for a coherent spatial arrangement and layout, mindful of the time-based dynamics of daily activities.

In comprehensive interior living room design, categorization is foundational. Spaces are classified by usage, life behaviors, spatial composition, environmental systems, and decorative furnishings. Systematic organization groups related elements within indoor spaces based on inherent connections and spatial order, forming a cohesive whole. Without a systematic framework, crucial elements may be overlooked. Effective system management involves subjective control with five key attributes: organizability, adaptability, dynamics, causality, and purpose. During living room design, qualitative analysis, logical deduction, and data-supported quantitative analysis are essential for ensuring the scientific validity and completeness of the design solution.

Innovative Design

Design creativity involves navigating and materializing the unknown, turning abstract notions into concrete forms and ideas. It draws upon four core skills: perception, memory, thought, and imagination, and entails the scientific use of knowledge and experience to forge new concepts and insights.

Fig 2.2:Creativity in design

In interior design, integrating environmental influences and human experiences is crucial, balancing functionality with aesthetic requirements. Top-notch designers disrupt traditional architectural and furnishing norms, weaving in cultural, social, economic, artistic, and scientific elements, oscillating between subjective and objective perspectives.
A designer's genius is displayed in commanding spatial arrangements and in the attention to detail with furnishings.

2.2 Interior Design Concepts and Techniques

Conceptualizing Living Room Interior Design

Conceptual Form Design

The essence of living room design lies in crafting a space that transcends simple visual duplication to offer an imaginative and aesthetically sensitive interpretation of reality. It's about creating an

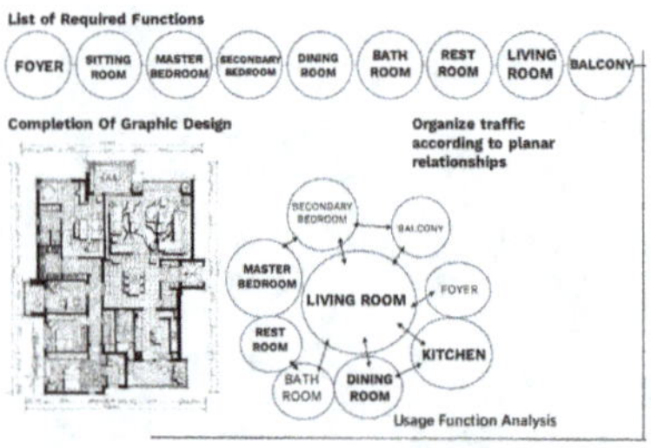

Fig 2.3:Interior space structure

Fig 2.4:Diagonal - Triangle The space is unique and requires more consideration of furniture placement and dead ends in the flow, etc

Fig 2.5:The arc-circle design is based on a unique house type, which makes full use of the shape of the space for lighting and functional design

ambiance that brings the room's spatial allure to life. Function, activity scale, materials, and the fusion of aesthetic and spiritual desires all shape the interior's form. At its core, it's the art of shaping space through the delicate balance of solid and void.

Primary spatial form emerges from enclosing areas with geometric clarity, employing furniture and partitions to delineate central zones, while secondary spaces are suggested through implied boundaries. The dynamic interplay of geometric forms - from the simplicity of lines and rectangles to the fluidity of curves - lends the space its character, adhering to underlying design principles.

Linear-Rectangular

This form, common in ancient Chinese architecture, emphasizes stability, guidance, symmetry, and adaptability, leading to a stable and atmospheric spatial design. It is often used in spaces like living rooms to increase visual depth and visually expand the area. However, an over-reliance on straight lines and rectangles can result in a monotonous design.

Slash-Triangle

Slash and triangle motifs are prevalent in structures with specialized functional significance, such as the East Wing of the National Gallery of Art in Washington, D.C., orchestrated by I.M. Pei. These motifs, dictated by site constraints, permeate both external and internal designs. Nonetheless, their usage in residential living spaces is rare due to potential dead space creation and necessary scrutiny of space utilization. With considered design, these motifs can escalate spatial aesthetics.

Arc-Circle

Arcs and circles add diversity, richness, and balance to living room designs. Although less common due to their perfect symmetry, circles create distinctive spatial forms and visuals. Arcs, larger in size, draw everything toward a central point and lessen the sense of location. Curved spaces, often a necessity due to space constraints, are excellent for crafting semi-open, communal areas such as living rooms or home offices.

Conceptualization

Conceptual design lays the groundwork for a project by crafting the visual and artistic vibe of a living room with various design elements. It encourages dwellers to ponder the practical aspects of their living space more thoughtfully.

The essence of the concept lies in the initial effort

In interior design, much like in fine art, the essence lies in conceptualization. A meticulous dive into the project's surroundings, purpose, materials, and aesthetics is imperative during the design phase. Establishing a solid conceptual foundation allows designers to visually map out their ideas through sketches. Key elements in shaping a space—its form, compositional principles, ambiance, current trends, art influences, architectural features, material choices, and decorative strategies—must be meticulously considered, transcending mere spatial and functional limits.

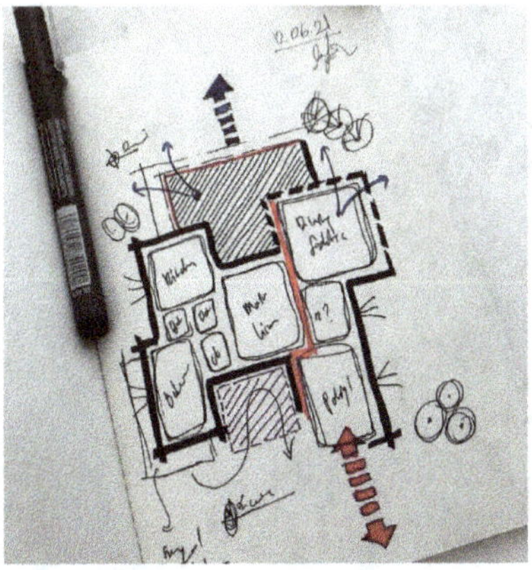

The Language of Interior Design Thinking in the Living Room

The visual language of living room interiors closely aligns with graphic expression, similar to code in IT, acting as a universal design language. Effective graphic expression aids in conveying design concepts and solutions. In living room design, graphic representation—mainly through sketches—is crucial at every stage. It provides a direct and quick method for visualizing ideas in the mind and developing them on paper, capturing the designer's creative sparks for further refinement.

During the conceptual phase, mind maps, often shown as bubble diagrams or logic trees, clarify the functional and spatial relationships within the living room. These tools promote broad, diverse thinking, leading to more sophisticated interior treatments. Designers then extract key information for comparative analysis, ultimately determining the design direction and objectives. Throughout the exploration and exchange of ideas, comprehensive thinking and design proposals are illustrated through floor plans, elevations, perspectives, and functional analyses, presenting a holistic view of the design logic and plan.

Fig 2.6: Concept sketches, through which observations and reflections are mapped out

2.3 Essentials of Living Room Layout

Fundamentals of Living Room Interior Design

Living room design meets occupant needs, considering different users, activities, behaviors, and aesthetics. It aims to satisfy both functional and emotional aspects of the space. Key design principles are: Highlighting spatial character, focusing on form and presentation, crafting spatial sequences, creating a visual focal point, and fostering innovation.

Emphasizing Spatial Character

Spatial character is primarily shaped by different modeling features. For instance, a traditional Chinese study should embody solemnity and symmetry, often utilizing regular shapes and layouts. In contrast, irregular shapes can create a casual, fluid atmosphere.

Table 2.1 Shape and characterization of space

	Space modeling features	Spatial characterization
Morphology of space	Regular geometric shapes: squares, circles, etc.	Solemn, solemn, smooth
	Irregular shapes: curve-based	Casual, free, fluid

Fig 2.7:Study room design According to the needs of the occupants can be empty and open, but also through the bookcases and other furniture to form a cordial atmosphere

Size of space	Higher floor heights and larger areas	Open and atmospheric
	Low floor height and small area	Intimate, oppressive
The order of space	Horizontal extension	Smooth, sprawling, open, peaceful
	Vertical extension	Visual guides, solemnity, sanctity, solemnity

Meeting residents' needs through adaptive spatial design

Space variations are vital in designing both vertical and horizontal areas, influencing dynamics and psychological balance. The arrangement of spaces—interspersed, enclosed, juxtaposed, or permeable—elicits various psychological reactions from occupants. Incorporating natural elements like greenery and water can enrich a space's dynamic nature.

For instance, during a Taipei apartment renovation, the aim was to improve space efficiency by removing unnecessary hallways. Analyzing movement patterns helped differentiate between dynamic and static zones. The vertically oriented spatial layout maximized visual flow in the limited space.

This method not only boosts space functionality but also fosters a more engaging and adaptive environment that responds to occupants' activities and moods.

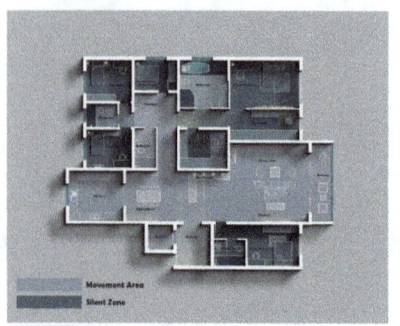

Fig 2.8:The flow lines in the action area are more penetrating and the space is open and free; each room in the quiet area has a separate entrance and is less interconnected

Focus on space sequence shaping

In interior design, each functional area within a space is unique yet interconnected, creating a dynamic coexistence that shapes the spatial sequence. This sequence can be structured as a simple chain or a more complex composite arrangement. During the design process, understanding how these spaces interact and influence the overall sequence is essential.

Single-chain spaces provide a clear functional flow, exemplified by the typical progression from the entrance where one changes shoes, to the bathroom to wash hands, to the kitchen to prepare dinner, and finally to the living room for relaxation after eating. This linear arrangement is straightforward but highly effective. While movement in single-chain spaces is coherent, visual breaks can be introduced through spatial divisions and furniture placement, allowing occupants to see only specific parts of the room, thus deepening the perceived interior depth of the living room.

Conversely, composite spaces are more intricate, offering a richer interplay of functions and forms. This complexity enhances the visual experiences for occupants as they navigate through the living room,

Fig 2.9:Segmentation of indoor dynamic and static zones can increase transitional space

contributing to a more holistic spatial perception.

Focus on spatial visual accents

In the cozy confines of a home, the living room demands a visual anchor or centerpiece that defines its distinctive spatial identity. Each nook within the living room benefits from having its own standout feature to steer the design. This point of interest not only elevates the visual appeal but also enriches the emotional ambiance of the room.

Crafting a visual centerpiece in the living room can be done using a tapestry of design tactics. Structurally, features like columns can be accentuated to act as sturdy visual pillars, enhanced by tweaks to the nearby architecture. Decoratively, the deliberate placement of artwork, wall decor, sculptures, and furniture can establish a visual hub. These elements, with their careful consideration of placement, shape, texture, color, illumination, and size, play pivotal roles in forging an engaging visual centerpiece for the living room.

Fig 2.10:Mutual combinations between the shapes of furniture, partitions, and accessories form a visual flow and a dynamic flow of change circulation

Techniques for Living Room Interior Arrangement

Planning and Styling Your Living Room Space

The visual charm of a living room's interior is felt through everyday interactions and observations within the space. The strategic placement of functional elements can yield a variety of aesthetic results. To satisfy the practical needs of its inhabitants, living room design can delve into aspects like spatial contrast and diversity, clear articulation and smooth transitions, transparency and depth, elevation shifts, and directional prompts. These thoughtful considerations amplify both the aesthetic and practical allure of the space.

Exploring Contrast and Variety in Living Spaces

Fig 2.11:Bake the visual focus of space through the strong contrast of color and material texture

Spatial contrasts can trigger various psychological reactions in residents. For example, moving from a bright, open living room to a cozy, dimly lit bedroom can boost a sense of comfort and safety. Designers can highlight these contrasts by playing with volume, shape, floor levels, and openness. Using distinct materials can heighten the contrast, whereas using uniform materials or patterns can soften it. Crafting these contrasts thoughtfully, by creating a rhythmic flow, ensures transitions feel deliberate and cohesive, enhancing the living experience without overwhelming. Incorporating geometric shapes like triangles and arcs, for instance, can escalate visual appeal and the overall sense of contrast.

Designing Seamless Spatial Transitions

Simply connecting two spaces without thoughtful consideration can lead to a disjointed and shallow feeling, stripping a room of its potential depth and coherence. Mastering spatial articulation and transition is key to not just improving a space, but also shaping the occupant's journey through it. Utilizing techniques like color variation, strategic furniture arrangement, and targeted lighting can significantly enhance these

Fig 2.12:Clearly dividing two different functional spaces by contrasting materials and light

transitions, bringing defined purpose and clarity to each area.

Elevating and Grounding Spaces through Design

Manipulating the elevation of certain zones within an interior can introduce height variations that act as subtle yet effective dividers for different functional areas. This strategy is especially beneficial in spaces like living rooms and bedrooms, where it not only enhances aesthetics but also boosts practicality and storage options. Ideal for compact lofts, this approach can also be cleverly used to showcase decorative elements.

Fig 2.13:Spatial transitions can be organized and differentiated in a variety of ways, including carpeting, furniture, lamps, and light sources

Navigating Spaces with Guided and Implied Boundaries

In the heart of the home, living room layouts are craftily arranged to direct guests, drawing their focus towards lively gathering areas, while keeping private quarters and storage out of the spotlight. This is artfully achieved by playing on innate human behaviors and the allure of a well-designed main space. Smart techniques range from the use of semi-open dividers that gently demand attention, to the guiding flow of walls and stairways. The arrangement of furniture in diverse shapes, sizes, and arrangements, along with thoughtful lighting, further navigates the eye and foot traffic, creating an intuitive and welcoming environment.

Fig 2.14:Spatial infiltration and hierarchy can be blocked by glass doors, screen peaks, etc. for flow while preserving visual circulation

Fundamentals of Apartment Interior Design

The essence of living room design is rooted in fundamental aesthetic and creative principles that govern human environments. Key concepts such as unity, harmony, balance, and rhythm are pivotal in crafting living spaces that resonate with both form and function. These elements ensure that living rooms are not only visually cohesive but also emotionally resonant, providing a harmonious backdrop for daily life.

Repetition and Gradation in Design

To dodge the dullness of overly uniform interiors, savvy designers often play with repetition, dotting spaces with wall art and home accessories that stick to a cohesive color palette. Such elements, when spaced with precision, lend a clear, orderly vibe to any room. Yet, it's the subtle shift of gradation—those incremental variations—that injects harmony and a dynamic visual appeal, keeping the eyes entertained and the spirit engaged.

Fig 2.15:Spatial elevation treatments can divide the nature of the space and create storage space through elevation differences

Harmony and Contrast: Balancing Acts in Design

The living room, a core hub for daily activities, demands a design that's engaging yet not overwhelming. Achieving this balance means weaving together elements like shape, color, and style, alongside consistent materials and textures, to create a unified visual narrative.

To inject vitality without tipping into chaos, skillful contrasts are key. In the living room, this could mean playing with dimensions—size, height, length—as well as introducing varied movements, densities, and lines. Juxtaposing cool and warm hues, along with mixing textures, can

Fig 2.16:Forming guidance and suggestion through spatial treatment of entrances

significantly elevate the room's aesthetic and ambiance, making it a more dynamic and enjoyable space.

Symmetry and Equilibrium in Design

Equilibrium and symmetry are foundational to creating visually stable interiors, drawing on aesthetic principles shaped by long-standing observations of nature. Unlike two-dimensional art, achieving balance in interiors requires considering the three-dimensional aspect of space.

Traditionally, Chinese architecture leverages symmetry to impart a sense of grandeur, stability, and formality in spaces, including apartments. In contrast, balance in interior design can be more dynamic, achieved through subtle variations. For example, in a living room, while the TV backdrop might be symmetrical, the accessories on either side can differ as long as they maintain a balanced look through consistent size, color, and placement. This approach ensures the space feels both stable and lively, offering a fresh take on traditional design principles.

Fig 2.17: When furniture materials tend to be uniform, they need to be contrasted in terms of shape, volume, height, and formation of streamlines

Rhythm and Rhyme in Design

Rhythm and meter, deeply entwined in their essence, play a pivotal role in the orchestration of design. Rhythm, with its roots in repetition, complexity, transformation, and reset, masterfully introduces variations in height, intensity, and contrast to create a spatial cadence. This rhythmic regularity, when skillfully applied to design, especially in living room interiors, manifests through changes in elements such as color and material.

Take, for instance, a partition grille that, while consistent in material and color, varies in density across different functional zones. This strategic distribution not only maintains a visual thread throughout the space but also infuses it with a lively, organic rhythm, making the space feel dynamic yet cohesive.

2.4 Contrasting Yet Complementary: Living Room and Architectural Design

Fig 2.18: Symmetry and equilibrium lead to a more stable space, and variations in detail make the space richer

Contrasting Elements: Residential Interior Design vs. Architectural Design

A common conundrum surfaces: '*How do architecture and interior design differ?*' Both fields revolve around crafting design solutions, yet they diverge in focus. Architects shape the building's very skeleton, the structural integrity and external features. In contrast, interior designers hone in on the inner tapestry, weaving together furniture, fixtures, and accessories to curate the desired ambiance and practicality within those spaces. The distinction boils down to three key areas.

Focus and Scale: A Study in Contrast

Architectural design operates on a grand scale, orchestrating the broader aspects of residential buildings that range from detached villas to sprawling high-rises. It's a realm where the timeless adage from the

Fig 2.19: Using partition walls, lighting, and furniture for spatial repetition to increase spatial rhythm and rhyme

Fig 2.20:Use of space and longevity in the architectural history domain

renowned skyscraper pioneer, Louis Sullivan, "*Form follows function*," rings true. Architecture dives into the macro level, tackling the building's integration with its environment, addressing traffic flow, and optimizing sunlight exposure.

Contrastingly, interior design narrows its lens to the micro, honing in on the specifics of living spaces. It's about tailoring the structural system to meld functionality with form, focusing on floor plans, spatial proportions, and the minutia of daily life, such as ensuring the accessibility of aisles and escape routes.

Living room design epitomizes this focus on the micro. It's not just about occupying a smaller physical area than architectural design but about a deep dive into the occupants' needs through detailed consultations. The aim? To craft spaces that aren't just functional but also aesthetically pleasing and psychologically comforting, leveraging lighting, color, and materials to cater to the occupants' well-being.

In essence, while architectural design sketches the broad strokes of a building's existence, interior design fills in the vibrant details, making each space not just livable but a sanctuary attuned to its inhabitants' lives.

Phases and Durability in Architecture vs. Interior Design

In the realm of building design, architecture sets the stage, laying the backbone for the subsequent phase of interior design. It creates the overall structure, with an eye towards future needs and potential renovations. Interior design then steps in to flesh out this skeleton, tailoring the inside to meet structural necessities and enhance functionality, often fine-tuning aspects that architecture didn't fully encapsulate.

With a lifespan often north of 50 years, buildings stand the test of time. Yet the rhythm of interior design is swift and adaptive, continuously molding to changes in occupants' lifestyles, emotional states, and other factors. The rate at which interiors evolve can be dramatic; everything from furniture rearrangement to substantial spatial modifications and upkeep happens at a brisk pace. For example, the arrival of a new family member can cause a family to entirely redo their functional layout and decor style in just a few years' time.

Distinct Roles: Architects and Interior Designers

In the world of design, architects and interior designers both bring a lot to the table. They're not just masters of the rulebook, knowing building codes like the back of their hand, they're also wizards at crunching numbers and bending over backward to meet client needs—all while keeping a sharp eye on the bottom line.

Architects are the maestros of the blueprint, the ones who dot the i's and cross the t's on the grand plan. They're in the trenches, often pounding the pavement at construction sites to make sure everything's up to snuff. Their day-to-day is a juggling act—huddling with clients, hashing out the nitty-gritty of designs, pinning down budgets, giving building regulations the once-over, shaking hands on deals with the heavy hitters, and playing detective on site.

Then you've got interior designers, the heart and soul of a space's inner life. They've got an eye for beauty and the know-how to make it happen. But it's not all about having a wild imagination; they've got to be sticklers for details and smooth talkers too. They're the folks clients cozy up to, laying their visions on the table, figuring out how to make every dollar count, tailoring their masterpieces to fit the bill, and always picking out the right stuff to make sure a space isn't just easy on the eyes but safe and sound too.

So, whether you're in it for the big picture or the intimate details, these pros have got the blueprint for success.

Synergies between Home Interior and Architectural Design

Architectural and interior design are essential, interconnected stages of a building project, sharing common goals and overlapping processes.

Maintaining Design Goal Consistency

The core aim of both interior and residential design is to meet the occupants' needs, such as a family desiring a secure, private, and well-lit home with good ventilation. This requires a seamless blend of architectural and interior elements, like a sturdy, closed exterior paired with an interior optimized for light and air, complemented by carefully placed furniture. This integration aligns with the design concept, fulfilling both functional and emotional needs.

Throughout the design process, clear communication is vital for designers to ensure architectural and interior styles complement each other, enhancing the overall aesthetic. In contrast, mismatched styles, even with ornate decorations, can result in a disjointed look. For instance, a modern minimalist exterior coupled with randomly chosen European or American interior elements, despite being rich, may not provide a visually and spiritually satisfying experience for the occupants.

The Spectrum of Influential Factors

Interior and architectural design must navigate the dual mandates of utility and aesthetics, addressing practical needs while embracing environmental, historical, and cultural nuances. This complex task marries form with function, civil engineering with creative vision. Take, for example, the divergent design philosophies of northern versus southern regions. Northern designs, like the traditional courtyard homes, leverage natural elements to protect against the elements, creating a comfortable microclimate—a principle still pertinent in contemporary design.

In the south, cities like Suzhou experience a humid, rainy climate, shaping architecture that mirrors the elegance of classical gardens, prioritizing intricate designs that maintain the integrity of residential living. Material choices, design techniques, and furnishings vary greatly from their northern counterparts here.

Despite these differences, both northern and southern design philosophies are deeply enmeshed with the local climate, environment, history, and socio-economic context. A home that truly resonates with its inhabitants, offering a sense of belonging and identity, can only emerge from a deep understanding of these diverse factors.

Fig 2.21:The building creates a free-flowing living environment through courtyards, terraces, vegetation, and window openings

Fig 2.22:The interior design is simple in terms of furniture and lighting, creating a sense of free flow

Fig 2.23:Natural environment is the biggest Influence on Homes

Seamless Fusion of Design and Construction

Creating a cohesive living room space demands a tight-knit collaboration between interior and architectural design, ensuring indoor and outdoor areas flow seamlessly. Key to this process is getting a handle on the homeowner's vision and actively translating it into a proactive design strategy.

Architects have the task of balancing curb appeal with interior utility. Overlooking the synergy between a home's façade and its inner sanctum can trigger a domino effect, where architectural oversights lead to extensive and costly overhauls. It's like building a house of cards only to have it toppled by the slightest misalignment. Thus, to avoid a house of corrections, it's prudent for architects and interior designers to work in lockstep from the get-go, fostering continuous dialogue and teamwork.

This collaborative spirit should extend into meticulous construction techniques, analytical rigor, and the use of simulations to predict outcomes. Such due diligence helps keep both design and functionality in sync, warding off any unwelcome surprises.

The scope of a residential project encompasses both construction and interior outfitting. Yet, differing perspectives and role limitations mean it's essential to hammer out the details of how these two phases interlink before breaking ground. This calls for iterative brainstorming sessions to safeguard the quality of the final abode.

The extent of an interior designer's involvement can swing widely based on the residence type. In detached villas, the designer's creativity must dovetail with the architect's blueprint and the homeowner's personal style. Conversely, in multi-unit dwellings like apartments or condos, the building's exterior sets the stage, and the interior designer has the latitude to maximize functionality and aesthetic potential within these parameters. This ensures that living areas, the heart of the home, deliver a full spectrum of comfort and amenities to residents.

Blending Residential Interiors with Architectural Design

Interior design and architectural design are two sides of the same coin, each contributing to a holistic approach that harmonizes with the environment and prioritizes human experience. Both fields are dedicated to not only meeting the practical needs of residents but also reflecting the local natural environment, geographical nuances, and cultural heritage.

By integrating these design elements into living rooms, we elevate both functionality and aesthetics, crafting spaces that are as beautiful as they are practical. This synergy creates a living space that is more than just a room—it's a comprehensive, cohesive environment that resonates with its inhabitants and surroundings.

In essence, the marriage of interior and architectural design is about telling a story through space. It's about weaving together the practical and the poetic, ensuring that every corner of a living room tells a tale of comfort, culture, and connection to the world outside.

Crafting Cohesion: The Art of Living Room Design Integration

Achieving a seamless blend of living room interior design with the wider residential architecture requires a keen eye for detail. It's essential to consider factors such as how we perceive the space visually, the psychological impact of the design, how the room is arranged, and the cultural influences at play. Paying attention to these details ensures the space is tailored to the occupant's needs, while also enhancing its visual and intrinsic appeal.

By striking this balance, we create living spaces that aren't just visually striking, but also deeply comforting and culturally resonant. The end goal is a living room that goes beyond aesthetics, offering a harmonious environment that truly feels like home.

Envisioning the Ideal Dwelling

Research shows that vision is fundamental to our perception of physical objects, and it plays a pivotal role in our experiences and emotions within a living space. The dimensions of the space, the architectural design, and the dynamic interaction of light and shadow significantly influence how we feel and interact within our homes. Understanding these elements can transform a house into a more harmonious and responsive environment that aligns with our senses and needs.

Blurring the Lines: Integrating Indoor and Outdoor Living

Integrating the interior design of a home with its exterior and surroundings can significantly enhance the spatial experience. By strategically employing architectural elements, materials, and colors, designers can forge a seamless transition between indoor and outdoor spaces, visually enlarging the interior realm.

A key strategy involves the continuous application of flooring and wall treatments. For instance, extending the same floor tiles or wood panels from an outdoor courtyard into the home, while subtly adjusting colors, textures, and materials, creates an intuitive and unified flow.

Glass elements, such as expansive windows and sliding doors, are pivotal in bridging the indoor-outdoor divide, fostering an open dialogue between the two environments. Aligning these features with the exterior view not only broadens the visual perspective but also ensures a cohesive integration of spaces. Opting for minimal frames maximizes visibility and strengthens this connection.

Fig 2.24:Visual guidance and visual extension through wall color and window openings and lighting

Echoing outdoor furniture styles and materials with those found indoors further blurs the lines between the two settings. Similarly, strategic lighting choices and the thoughtful placement of indoor plants can soften the distinction between inside and outside, promoting a sense of continuity and spatial harmony.

Elevating the Visual Experience of Interior Spaces

When you're working with a building whose exterior is set in stone, the key to a cohesive interior lies in making the living room's design sing in harmony with the building's overall architecture. Especially in cases where space is at a premium, it's crucial to aim for a design that feels balanced and sensory-rich, perfectly in tune with the spatial limits and

Fig 2.25:Smaller spaces designed to create a visual experience through spatially layered lighting

Fig 2.26:Light-colored furniture, minimalist modeling star space youthfulness, to meet the psychological needs of the occupants

In more intimate areas like bedrooms and bathrooms, opting for a compact design can introduce a comforting sense of enclosure. Contrastingly, the living room offers a canvas for strategic creativity. Implementing thoughtful partitions can cleverly navigate the building's constraints, amplifying the space's visual appeal.

This approach not only ensures the interior design feels proportionate and engaging but also weaves a seamless aesthetic thread throughout the home, making every square inch count.

The Psychology of Home: Navigating Residential Spaces

Each home is a personal retreat, tailored to its inhabitants, even when the exterior architecture follows a uniform style. The crux lies in the interior design, which must be personalized to meet the unique lifestyles and preferences of the residents. Crafting a space isn't just about achieving visual flow or maximizing square footage; it's fundamentally about nurturing an emotional connection between the home and its occupants.

The marriage between a home's physical aspects and the psychological comfort of those within is essential. This union is reflected through careful selection and customization of design elements—like patterns, furniture size and shape, color palettes, and materials. These choices are thoughtfully aligned not just with aesthetic preferences but also with the residents' age, gender, and profession, ensuring that each space resonates emotionally.

Residential interior design's emotional depth is deeply intertwined with the harmony of décor and architectural character. Strategic use of colors and textures can dramatically reinvent a space, elevating the ambiance and playing a pivotal role in the overall home experience.

The Art of Living Space: Designing with Purpose

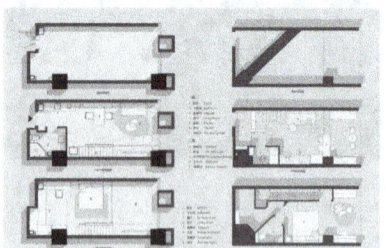

Fig 2.27:Floor plan layout

Fig 2.28:Furniture forms newtown functional area flow line

Space organization is the backbone of both architecture and interior design, essential for crafting a living environment that is both cohesive and functional. This discipline involves a comprehensive strategy to blend diverse functions within a space, ensuring a smooth and orderly experience for its inhabitants. By viewing architectural design, interior layout, and construction as interdependent components, a logical and coherent spatial arrangement emerges.

Upon entering a well-organized living space, each area is purposefully designed, yet these functional zones are interconnected, akin to chapters in a book that weave together under a central theme—the primary function of the space. This narrative unfolds seamlessly, with areas interweaving and overlapping to create a sense of harmony and unity. The strategic positioning of these zones not only facilitates smooth movement and activities but also enhances the experiential and comfort aspects of the living environment.

Spatial organization typically mirrors the natural flow of human activities, transitioning from public areas to more private spaces like bedrooms and bathrooms. The layout can greatly vary depending on the architectural blueprint, leading to diverse configurations such as single-axis, dual-axis, or branching patterns, each offering a unique spatial experience tailored to the inhabitants' needs.

Integration of natural landscapes

Since time immemorial, architecture and the natural landscape have been intertwined, each shaping the other's presence. This relationship is especially pronounced in residential design, where incorporating elements like mountains, forests, and evergreens, along with crafting nature-inspired landscapes, enhances the living environment's comfort.

The artful fusion of outdoor landscapes with architectural forms helps to dissolve the separation between inside and outside, providing inhabitants with a profound connection to nature. This enriches not just the residents' quality of life and aesthetic enjoyment but also plays a key role in urban greening. It stretches the spatial experience and elevates the living environment, fostering a balanced coexistence between humans, nature, and the urban tapestry.

Indoor natural landscapes serve a crucial decorative function, often surpassing the impact of their outdoor counterparts in refining living spaces and fostering a warm ambiance. Choosing and positioning indoor plants should be in harmony with the external environment and climate, taking into account factors like plant size, shape, and variety. It's also essential to consider the inhabitants' preferences and the intended mood for different rooms. For example, study spaces benefit from the calm elegance of small branches and shade-tolerant miniature potted plants that mirror the occupants' sophisticated tastes. In contrast, living rooms and other communal areas should feature plants strategically placed in frequently used spots, complementing the room's activities without causing disruption, and matching the overall spatial design.

An effective indoor natural landscape strategy not only aligns with the outdoor setting but also observes spatial organization principles, crafting a balanced and dynamic natural display that resonates throughout the home.

Fig 2.29:Residential atrium plantscapes combined with interior materials to create an integrated atmosphere

Interior and Furniture Integration

Furniture is the cornerstone of any living room, setting the tone for style, substance, and functionality. To achieve a unified aesthetic, furniture must be in concert with the interior space, as mismatched pieces can jar the room's harmony.

The tactile experience provided by furniture materials is immediate and influential. These materials should not only blend with the interior environment but also offer variety in texture and appearance. For example, while linen is a go-to choice for sofa upholstery, it can also feature in other decor aspects, weaving a consistent visual theme throughout the space.

The structure of furniture should mirror the home's overall design and resonate with the lifestyle of its inhabitants. In a modern Chinese setting, the visible mortise-and-tenon joints pay homage to age-old artistry, echoing the ethos of 'unity of man and nature' and creating a space that encourages tranquility. In smaller abodes, versatile, space-saving furniture is a game-changer, allowing the environment to morph and cater to a range of activities.

Beyond basic utility, furniture should promote spatial fluidity. It can function as a subtle divider of areas, direct the room's use, and soften the lines between different parts of the home. Take a bookshelf: it can

Fig 2.30:Indoor Furniture Integration: Furniture tends to be folded and movable according to functional needs

cleverly separate a study from the living area, forging two distinct but visually interlinked environments within a modest footprint, preserving an open feel and a consistent visual narrative.

cultural environment

China's vast and varied landscape, coupled with its rich tapestry of ethnic diversity, presents a fertile ground for architectural and interior design to flourish, infusing spaces with unique national and regional identities. The essence of these designs lies not just in their functionality and aesthetic appeal but in their ability to encapsulate the cultural essence and significance of the spaces they inhabit.

In crafting these environments, materials, colors, and patterns are more than mere elements; they are tools to echo local cultural subtleties, weaving a cohesive narrative that resonates with the broader urban cultural landscape. This approach not only accentuates the distinctiveness of the interior but also fosters a sense of place and cultural continuity. For example, incorporating preserved architectural elements and reimagining residential spaces through decorative construction can stir a poignant sense of historical connection and cultural reverence.

The hallmark of successful architecture in China is its seamless fusion of contemporary design and lifestyle with cultural and historical threads, achieving a harmonious synthesis that speaks to both the past and the present. This delicate balance ensures that each space tells a story, enriching the lives of those who inhabit it with a deep sense of cultural belonging and pride.

Fig 2.31:Formation of unique interior design elements based on the cultural rows of the site

Bridging Interiors and Architecture: The Key to Cohesive Living Spaces

When architects and interior designers join forces, the result is a symphony of functionality where the building's external and internal spaces dance in harmony. This collaborative approach ensures that the stylistic elements of the entire living space are amplified, fostering innovative transformations that cater to residents' needs while enhancing spatial quality and overall life satisfaction.

To avoid the pitfalls of post-construction alterations, it's essential to weave architectural and interior design together from the outset. This proactive approach not only prevents costly and disruptive modifications but also allows for a thorough exploration of needs, conserving resources and ensuring the structural integrity and safety of the living space.

The integration of design disciplines also invigorates related industries, from building materials to furniture and electrical services. By fostering a comprehensive perspective, this holistic approach ensures a cohesive design journey from the exterior façade to the interior finishes, mitigating the risks of disjointed industry involvement and stimulating market vitality through robust collaboration.

Embracing the principle of 'unity with nature' is paramount in living room design. The careful selection of eco-friendly and healthy materials not only enhances the natural aesthetic but also fosters a harmonious coexistence with the environment. Materials that are toxic or emit radiation detract from this natural beauty and pose health risks. For instance, incorporating untreated wood, like the tactile and aromatic

Fig 2.32:Indoor and outdoor style unification

walnut, strengthens the occupants' connection to nature, promoting relaxation and well-being. However, mindful of the ecological impact and the long growth cycle of natural wood, designers must balance their use to avoid environmental harm while striving to enrich the occupants' quality of life.

The Principle of Maximizing Gains and Minimizing Risks

Nan Huaijin, a revered scholar, once said, '*A culture that has stood the test of time carries its own truths.*' Indeed, the ancient principles of Feng Shui, often dismissed as mere superstition, are finding echoes in contemporary scientific discourse. The '*unfavorable*' elements that Feng Shui advises us to evade can arise from both the forces of nature and human engineering. Take, for example, the Bank of China Tower in Hong Kong. Designed by the esteemed architect I.M. Pei, the building originally sparked Feng Shui controversy for its sharp angles, which were believed to symbolize '*financial drain.*' To counter this, Pei cleverly introduced two leaning fountains at the building's base, which fostered a sense of '*financial flow*' and overturned the negative connotations to ones of prosperity. This alteration played a dual role: it altered the building's water circulation and shifted the psychological perception of the space.

Within the intimate confines of interior design, the influence of Feng Shui is profound, guiding everything from the avoidance of sharp edges, known as '*poison arrows,*' to the strategic placement of bathrooms. Feng Shui links room placement to celestial bearings and their associated implications, like the inauspicious '*greedy wolf*' star. These practices are deeply entrenched in human behavior and habitat. For instance, placing a bathroom in the center of a home—considered the core of the dwelling—can disrupt waste removal, natural lighting, and the seamless flow of everyday life. Such insights weave together the strands of ancient knowledge with the fabric of contemporary living, creating a tapestry that balances time-honored tradition with practicality.

Feng Shui Meets Aesthetics: Elevating Living Room Design

Traditional Chinese aesthetics, woven through with the threads of Feng Shui philosophy, stand as a cornerstone of Chinese architectural thought. These aesthetics champion 'harmony between humans and nature,' melding the beauty of the natural world with human creativity to shape spaces that delight the senses and nurture the soul. In residential design, this approach goes beyond simply aligning a structure within its natural setting. It involves crafting an interior that balances straight lines with fluid movement, achieves a state of equilibrium and solidity, and captures a rhythmic grace that resonates on an emotional level. These principles create an ambiance that is not only visually striking but also promotes a profound sense of well-being.

The Beauty of Straight and Curve

The principles of 'curvature' and 'straightness' in Feng Shui draw inspiration from the natural watercourses of mountain landscapes, symbolizing the dynamic interplay of yin and yang—their ebb and flow, and the dance between motion and stillness. Mountains, inherently static,

Fig 2.33: Doorway design and partition design can adopt more diversified shapes and means; plants are a good accent element for the vitality of space

acquire a dynamic essence through their curves, reflecting the philosophy that '*the mountain stands still, yet harbors dynamic potential.*' Conversely, water, a dynamic force in Feng Shui, achieves a serene stillness, embodying the concept that '*the water flows, yet its beauty lies in its tranquility.*'

In traditional Chinese gardens, this dynamic aesthetic is masterfully expressed through winding paths and the seamless integration of varying vistas, imbuing the landscape with life. This aesthetic carries profound implications for contemporary living room design, guiding layout strategies and the choice of decorative elements. For example, by viewing straight lines as '*static*' and curves as '*dynamic,*' designers can strategically employ partitions or wall sections to creatively divide small spaces or enhance the fluidity within a room. This approach not only fulfills the functional need for space division but also enlivens the area, transforming the potential for movement and expanding the spatial experience, thereby infusing the room with vitality.

The beauty of harmony and stability

Anchored in the Confucian ideal of '*centering,*' Feng Shui's guiding principle promotes a symbiotic relationship between humanity and the natural world. It calls for a seamless integration of elements—trees, flowers, mountains, rivers, and flowing waters—into an ancient site's design that sings with harmony. The Feng Shui approach is not one-size-fits-all but a careful study of the land, tailored to the unique needs of its inhabitants to foster a stable and enduring relationship between people, their homes, and the environment.

Fig 2.34: Forming spaces and differences through aesthetic design prototypes

The Feng Shui ethos of '*harmony without uniformity*' sidesteps the mundane pursuit of sheer geometric balance or repetitive axial symmetry. Particularly in northern traditional Chinese architecture, while a central axis may signify hierarchy, the true essence lies in celebrating '*unity in diversity.*' This design philosophy weaves together a tapestry of varied, lively elements that strike a dynamic balance between yin and yang, offering rich complexity in lieu of simple repetition. Similar to a symphony's diverse notes that blend to create a cohesive, melodious whole, architectural spaces evolve continually, facilitating an interplay between the tangible and the intangible to craft habitats that cater to human well-being.

The aesthetic of harmony and stability stems from the deliberate orchestration of dynamic components, fostering visual and spiritual serenity in design. This equilibrium aligns with human lifestyles and spatial sensibilities, ensuring that spaces are not only functionally apt but also resonate with residents on a more profound, experiential plane.

The beauty of mood and rhythm

In the realm of traditional Chinese aesthetics, the true essence of beauty is often found within the context. Echoing Lao Tzu's sentiment, '*the Tao that can be described is not the eternal Tao,*' there lies a nuanced interplay between the familiar and the unique. Architecture and interior design transcend mere physical spaces, embodying a '*qi charm*' that marries the allure of objects with their environment. This concept of beauty goes beyond the physical, challenging us to grasp its intangibility through intuition rather than explicit definition. The ephemeral grace of mood and rhythm, pillars of Chinese tradition, invites exploration in architectural marvels like classical gardens and imperial mausoleums.

In the domain of living room interior design, the dialogue between mood and rhythm transforms a space into an experiential canvas, reminiscent of the emotive power of poetry, the depth of a landscape painting, or the melody of a song. These elements collectively refine the spatial experience. Designers employ a holistic approach, leveraging spatial divisions, furniture arrangement, decor selection, plant life, lighting, and more, to cultivate a unique atmosphere that resonates with the inhabitants' aesthetic tastes and lifestyle. For instance, a rustic style evokes a sense of simplicity and authenticity, whereas a modern Chinese motif offers a serene, minimalist retreat. Through these meticulous design choices, a living room becomes more than just a space—it becomes a testament to the nuanced art of living, tailored to the individual's essence.

Fig 2.35:Interior design is not necessarily full of furniture everywhere, it is more important to grasp the mood and rhythm

The Structure and Purpose of Living Room Interiors

1. Variety and Boundaries of Living Room Spatial Designs
2. Spatial Function and Layout of the Living Room Interior

Chapter 3: The Structure and Purpose of Living Room Interiors

3.1 Variety and Boundaries of Living Room Spatial Designs

In designing living rooms, we draw upon the distinct purposes and inherent features of various living areas. Our selection and organization of designs focus on optimizing the layout, dimensions, materials, and finishes. This approach is designed to boost both the practicality and the visual allure of living room spaces.

Private Sanctuaries in the Living Room

Within the living room's embrace, private nooks like bedrooms, bathrooms, and studies offer a retreat for extended solitude and reflection. Designed with inward-focused symmetry, these areas foster a cocoon of centeredness. The carefully chosen boundaries of these spaces heighten a sense of safety, creating a personal haven within the home.

Fig 3.1:Private sanctuaries in the living room

Open and Airy Spaces

Open spaces in the living room breathe life into the home with their outward focus, offering a sense of freedom rather than confinement. These areas are designed to encourage movement and interaction, facilitated by an orientation that guides the eye and a rhythmic layout that pulses with life. Often, these spaces feature at least one open side, allowing for a seamless flow between inside and outside, as is common in living rooms that embrace an open-plan design. The exterior walls are deliberately less restrictive, with varied shapes and designs that add depth and dynamism. Such design choices allow for a harmonious blend with the outside world, promoting an exchange of spaces that crafts a "*four-dimensional space*," where the dimensions of space and time are intricately intertwined.

Fig 3.2:Open and airy spaces

Fluid and Imaginary Spaces

The magic of virtual mobility in design is captured through visual hints and psychological triggers within the space, using interior elements and decor to stir the imagination. This approach symbolically segments the area without traditional barriers, fostering an open vista and encouraging the seamless blending of spaces. A prime example is the main indoor balcony, which can be subtly differentiated through varied materials yet remain connected via transparent elements like glass, ensuring a continuous visual narrative.

Fig 3.3:Fluid and imaginary spaces

Strategic Space Qualification

qualification is crucial for infusing it with purposeful utility. This process harnesses abstract design elements—points, lines, and planes—to sculpt the area into a functional and meaningful environment.

Crafting Spatial Dimensions

To define space horizontally, subtle techniques are key. Enhancing spatial flow can involve creative top and bottom surface treatments—think altering floor levels, carving out mezzanine areas, or redefining ceiling space. These tactics are instrumental in molding the room's ambiance and character.

In Japan, where homes are often compact, horizontal space is artfully maximized to ensure both functionality and a tranquil enclosure. Vertical boundaries come with varying degrees of separation; full walls provide privacy and insulation, while partial barriers maintain an open feel, allowing for better spatial flow. Both approaches typically employ linear and planar elements to achieve their desired effect.

Fig 3.4:Crafting spatial dimensions japanese house

Centralized and Bounded Spaces

Space configurations, influenced by their design and human interaction, are classified into two types: centralized or bounded.

Centralized spaces create a focal point, forming a ring-like area that emanates from a central element, achieved through visual and psychological cues. This approach uses elements such as sculptures and lighting to subtly define boundaries, relying on their form, placement, texture, color, and volume to suggest the space's limits without rigid demarcation.

Bounded spaces, conversely, enhance the utility of a single area by strategically dividing it, either horizontally or vertically, to add layers and functionality. For instance, in many apartments, the kitchen and dining areas are integrated. Here, localized divisions like wall openings or glass partitions create soft boundaries that maintain an open flow, while flexible partitions such as curtains offer movable or adjustable space divisions.

Fig 3.5:Centralized and bounded spaces

Merging Spaces in the Living Room

Crafting Cohesive Spaces in the Living Room

The living room is the Swiss Army knife of home spaces, serving a plethora of functions in a resident's day-to-day hustle. It's where life's threads weave together. So, it's paramount that the living room's diverse areas blend without missing a beat. Crafting such a space means piecing together different zones with intention, ensuring they gel for smooth sailing and practical use, all while upping the ante on the living experience.

Integrated Spatial Relationships

(1)Intermingled Space: This concept involves the fusion of spaces,

Fig 3.6:Intermingled space

Fig 3.7:Adjacent space

such as direct connections, space amalgamation, and functional delineation are employed. For instance, a living room might incorporate an indoor atrium or transition effortlessly to an outdoor space, utilizing glass partitions for visual consistency while preserving separate zones. Elevated platforms can further blend spaces, fostering the integration of indoor and natural elements.

(2)Adjacent Space: This arrangement is prevalent in apartment layouts, characterized by walls, columns, furniture placements, and ceiling height variations. In contemporary living room designs, physical barriers are often reduced to boost spatial transparency and evoke a sense of expansiveness, thereby maximizing utility. When linking various functional zones within a communal area, subtle shifts in decor and furniture configurations are favored, particularly in compact spaces. In expansive areas, the manipulation of space dimensions and shapes can steer movement and define functions.

Strategies for Crafting Space

To elevate both the beauty and utility of your living room, consider these effective design techniques for spatial arrangement:
(1)Geometry in Design: Leverage basic geometric shapes—rectangles, triangles, polygons, alongside circles and ellipses—to forge a space that's both orderly and visually compelling.
(2) Harmonious Grids: Apply a grid system that crisscrosses both vertically and horizontally, introducing a sense of balance and proportion. This method helps in defining the scales and forms within the space.
(3) Micro and Macro Perspectives: Tackle design from both close-up and wide-angle lenses. While each functional zone within the living room stands as its unique entity, their interconnectivity should echo a cohesive style and narrative. Adopting this comprehensive view ensures fluidity and prevents a piecemeal look.

Fig 3.8:Geometry in design

(4)Spatial Manipulation: During the layout planning, fine-tune the dimensions of various sections by either expanding or reducing them, aiming for an optimal blend of function and aesthetic harmony. For example, adjusting the sizes of the guest room and living room can better distinguish their individual characteristics while ensuring they complement each other.

Crafting Harmony: The Golden Ratio in Living Room Design

Proportion and Scale

Fig 3.9:Harmonious grids

The ideas of proportion and scale in design are steeped in the classical traditions of geometry and mathematics, gifts from the ancient Greeks and Romans. They introduced the "*golden ratio*," embodying a logical beauty that echoes the aesthetic harmony found in nature and revered by scientists alike. This principle is a cornerstone for architects and designers, guiding them to forge spaces that are visually balanced and in tune.

In interior design, the golden ratio plays a pivotal role, shaping the ideal dimensions for furniture, decorations, and the entire room's both the room's functionality and its aesthetic charm, creating an environment that's not just easy on the eyes but also a haven of comfort and utility.

Scale and Proportion in Composition

The allure of indoor spaces is largely dictated by the artful arrangement of interface elements, which shape both planar and interface aesthetics. Drawing from mathematical concepts and inspired by Mondrian's geometric masterpieces, planar aesthetics employs rectangles of diverse proportions and scales, coupled with color variations, to craft visually captivating designs. Conversely, interface aesthetics hones in on the dimensions of the space, the weight of lines, and the spacing between elements, leveraging these to forge a balanced composition.

In the realm of interior design, these principles are instrumental in orchestrating the layout of space, ensuring that both the two-dimensional surfaces and the three-dimensional components collaborate seamlessly to produce a unified and aesthetically gratifying environment. By meticulously applying scale and proportion, designers sculpt spaces that are not only visually compelling but also functionally adept.

Scale and Ideology

To adhere to ergonomic standards, the planning of spaces must carefully account for how human activities blend with the surrounding environment. The configuration and elevation of a room profoundly impact individuals' behaviors and mental states. For example, the design of bedrooms, bathrooms, and studies with slightly lower ceilings can foster a sense of intimacy and security, embracing occupants with a cozy enclosure. On the flip side, dining and living areas benefit from higher ceilings, ensuring the space feels open and unrestrictive during social gatherings or relaxation.

Fig 3.10:Spatial proportion and scale

In the world of interior design, grasping these spatial nuances is key to creating settings that not only serve their practical purposes but also promote emotional well-being. Tailoring the scale and ceiling height to the function of each space allows designers to cultivate a sense of ease and psychological refuge, thereby elevating the living experience.

Design of Movement

In the dance of interior design, spatial fluidity takes center stage, closely intertwined with the rhythm of movement and the sweep of visual continuity. Such fluidity is defined by a seamless blend of visual and kinetic energy, sparked by the occupants' daily ballet of activities. The core mission of architecture is to cater to the needs of its residents, ensuring the created spaces resonate with and support the ebb and flow of human life.

Fig 3.11:Spatial proportion and scale

A thoughtful arrangement of pathways doesn't just streamline the choreography of daily motion; it also elevates the inhabitant's mental journey through their domestic landscape. Through the mindful crafting of these movement corridors, interior designers strike a and wellbeing.

Reasonable Layout of Flow Lines

In the unseen ballet of indoor movement, streamlines serve as the invisible threads that guide the dance of daily life, crucial for boosting both the functionality and the energy of a space. A smartly configured flow line network promotes ease of access, ensuring that paths to each area are clear and straightforward, cutting down on needless wandering. This planning takes into account the unique dynamics of flow in both private and communal areas, adapting to diverse needs and activities.

The crafting of flow lines should mimic water's adaptability, shaping itself to fit its surroundings. In the context of living spaces, the potential for seamless movement can be enhanced through thoughtful partitioning and the strategic placement of entryways.

Take, for example, a renovation project in a Canadian high-rise condo where the designer preserved the original layout's accessibility while minimizing the use of solid barriers. Furniture and curved partitions were employed instead, boosting the area's openness and adaptability. The introduction of curved walls not only injects aesthetic charm but also gently guides the eye, adding layers of flexibility and intrigue to the space, making every turn a discovery.

Psychological Impact of Streamlining

Fig 3.12:Space flow lines

In the art of space design, psychological nuances are critical, shaping how dwellers engage with their surroundings. Artistic touches, such as the strategic use of color contrasts or gradients, thoughtful lighting schemes, and the infusion of natural light, can discreetly choreograph movement and behavior. These elements not only set the tone for different zones but also subtly steer movement, deepening the psychological experience.

Echoing Le Corbusier's belief that "*Architecture is the masterly, correct and magnificent play of masses brought together in light*," manipulating light's intensity, warmth, and coolness adds layers of subtlety and depth to spatial guidance. This approach enriches the psychological impact of interiors, ensuring that design not only serves practical needs but also harmonizes with the emotional and psychological health of its inhabitants.

3.2 Spatial Function and Layout of the Living Room Interior

Communal Active Living Space

The living room stands out as the heart of the home, a private retreat from the bustle of public places like malls or theaters. It's a cozy haven for family time, socializing, entertainment, and unwinding, embracing a variety of activities. This area, encompassing the living space, foyer, and dining area, is key to nurturing family bonds and harmonious relations.

The design and utility of these shared zones within the living room should mirror the family's lifestyle, composition, and interests, tailored room into an inviting and versatile nucleus for both the household and visitors.

Fireplace

Characteristics

The living room is the linchpin of domestic life, often synonymous with a family room, and is the stage for family interactions, welcoming guests, and hosting group activities. It commands a prominent position in the home, embodying the homeowner's personal style, taste, and public persona.

Functionality

This space is tailored for gatherings, entertainment, family time, relaxation, and enjoying media. Designed to be open and connected, it flows into other home areas like the dining room, bedrooms, and balconies, making it the central node of domestic activity.

Design Principles

A "*core and satellites*" layout typifies living room interior design. For example, centering around a main seating area, it might be flanked by specialized zones for reading, enjoying tea, dining, or listening to music – each space echoing the inhabitants' personal style and preferences.

Furniture Layout

Essential living room furnishings include sofas, coffee tables, side tables, a TV, and speakers, addressing basic functional requirements. Arrangement should define primary and secondary zones, offering a sense of enclosure without overcrowding. The layout must ensure fluidity, with a clear passageway of 600mm to 900mm between pieces. As the home's thoroughfare, it's vital to keep walkways open, particularly around the perimeter. The secondary spaces should sport just enough practical furniture to avoid upstaging the main gathering area, maintaining its status as the room's centerpiece.

Fig 3.13:Fireplace decorations

Fig 3.14:Fireplace layout

Front Door

Characteristics

The foyer, or entryway, acts as a gateway, bridging the divide between the public exterior and the private interior of a home. Its design can range from a closed, intimate nook to a semi-open space, tailored to the home's layout and the inhabitants' lifestyle.

Functionality

This transitional zone is crucial for a seamless shift from the outside world to the sanctuary of home. It's equipped with practical features like shoe racks, key hooks, and storage for umbrellas and bags, often elegantly consolidated into sleek entrance and shoe cabinets in modern homes.

Fig 3.15:Front door design

Fig 3.16:Front door design

Fig 3.17:Enclosed dining room

with strategic placement of furniture, screens, or partitions that guard against prying eyes into the living area. This is especially beneficial when managing brief interactions, such as receiving deliveries or greeting guests, preserving a sense of seclusion and minimizing disruption to the home's private quarters.

As the initial showcase of the home's interior, the foyer's design should resonate with the overall style and ambiance, ensuring that each decorative touch harmonizes with the broader aesthetic of the residence.

Design Principles

Entryway design can be broadly classified into hard and soft approaches.Hard designs employ either solid or semi-transparent partitions. Solid barriers, like full-height walls, completely obstruct views into the living space, potentially limiting natural light and creating a sense of confinement in compact spaces. Semi-transparent partitions, such as half walls, screens, or glass, offer glimpses into the home while preserving privacy, commonly used in smaller homes to avoid a cramped atmosphere.

Soft designs concentrate on material, form, and decorative finishes. These elements should be kept uncomplicated to emphasize utility and blend with the overall interior design. Strategies include employing diverse ceiling shapes for spatial orientation, using contrasting wall and flooring materials or colors to demarcate areas, and strategically placing an entrance cabinet and decor to create a visual anchor point.

Dining Room, Kitchen

Characteristics

The dining room and kitchen serve as the epicenter of home life, each playing its unique role. While the dining room often acts as an extension of the living room for meals and socializing, the kitchen asserts itself as a standalone haven for culinary creation.

Functionality

The dining room's essence lies in hosting meals and fostering conversations, setting the stage for family bonding and entertainment. The kitchen, dedicated to the art of cooking, becomes more versatile with additions like wine cabinets, bars, and specialized stations for preparing various cuisines. These enhancements not only cater to the culinary preferences of the household but also elevate the overall lifestyle and activity diversity within the home.

Design Principles

Kitchen design should champion ergonomics, focusing on comfort and efficiency for enduring culinary endeavors. The ideal countertop stands 150mm higher than the user's wrist, while wall-mounted storage should hover between 1700mm to 1800mm for optimal accessibility.

The architecture of these spaces should complement the culinary open designs, inspired by Western dining trends and modern appliance innovations, strike a balance by using bars or partial walls to mitigate smoke without full separation. Open kitchens, free from barriers, foster a seamless integration with living spaces, making them a favorite in compact homes and among fans of Japanese or European culinary styles.

Consideration for the psychological impact of dining environments is paramount. Proper lighting and color schemes can significantly influence the dining ambiance. Natural light is preferred in kitchens for better ventilation, complemented by strategic overhead lighting to enhance task visibility. Boosting light intensity judiciously can make meals more visually appealing and cooking more pleasurable. Employing warm hues such as red and yellow can invoke appetite but should be applied with restraint to maintain a comforting, not overwhelming, space.

Fig 3.18:Semi-Open dining room

Privacy and Independence in Living Spaces

Private and independent zones within a home are meticulously crafted to meet the personal needs of its inhabitants, including areas for rest, dressing, and bathing, typically represented by bedrooms and bathrooms. The design philosophy behind these spaces is rooted in a deep understanding of individual physiological and psychological needs, coupled with personal aesthetic inclinations. The objective is to create an environment that not only ensures privacy and a sense of security but also provides enhanced comfort and the autonomy to self-regulate without the intrusion of external influences. This approach allows each family member to retreat into their own personal haven, fostering a harmonious balance between togetherness and individual space.

Fig 3.19:Open kitchen

Bedrooms

Characteristics

The bedroom is the epitome of personal space, a haven designed for undisturbed activities such as sleep, relaxation, and private moments.

Functionality

As lifestyles become more diverse, bedrooms are transforming to include multifunctional elements that cater to different user groups, considering age, gender, and occupation. For example, integrating a study within the bedroom can be a boon for writers and freelancers, providing a seamless transition from work to rest.

Design Principles

Functional Convenience: The cornerstone of bedroom design is to create a restful environment. This involves aligning furniture dimensions and storage solutions with user needs for optimal comfort. The master bedroom, used most frequently, can also incorporate entertainment and audiovisual elements for added convenience.

Privacy and Independence: Ensuring privacy is essential for a comfortable retreat. This is achieved through enhanced sound insulation

Fig 3.20:Bedroom design

Fig 3.21: Bedroom feature addition design

Fig 3.22: Children's room design

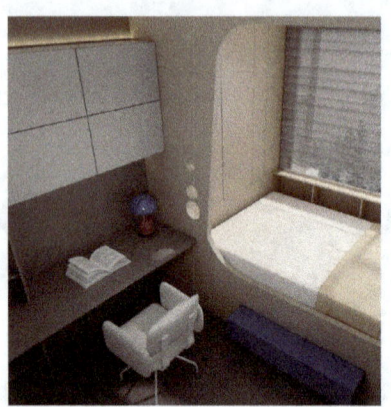

Fig 3.23: Children's room design

Fig 3.24: Sanitary spaces design

transparent materials like glass. Window placement should also consider the proximity of neighboring buildings.

Atmospheric Comfort: Crafting a soothing atmosphere involves careful decorative and lighting choices. Harmonious color schemes and soft lighting can minimize visual stress and amplify aesthetic appeal. Natural light is prized for its ability to enhance the sense of space, while indoor lighting should be versatile, with primary and secondary sources strategically positioned to suit various activities.

Tailoring to Children's Preferences

Children's bedrooms should inspire creativity and positive values through engaging spaces and decor. Incorporating interactive elements like whiteboards or cork boards can encourage expression and imagination. While rich colors stimulate creativity, they should be balanced to ensure they do not disrupt rest or visual comfort. Gender preferences also play a role in color choices and room decor.

Adapting to Children's Developmental Needs

Security: Opt for eco-friendly, non-toxic materials such as wood flooring and hemp wallpaper to create a safe environment. A warm, inviting design can help alleviate feelings of isolation, and ample lighting can diminish nighttime fears.

Growing Space: Furniture should be modular and adjustable to adapt to physical and psychological growth. This flexibility ensures the room remains relevant and functional as children's interests and body structures change over time.

Sanitary Spaces (Toilets and Bathrooms)

Multifunctionality

Today's bathrooms go beyond basic needs, offering a sanctuary for various activities from the daily essentials of washing and toileting to luxurious moments of reading, sipping on a favorite beverage, or indulging in audio-visual entertainment during a relaxing bath. As living standards soar, the demand for bathrooms to serve as multifaceted spaces has become the norm.

Core Design Principles

Privacy: A top priority in bathroom layout is maintaining privacy. Strategic placement of the bathroom door is crucial, ensuring it's not in direct sight from communal areas such as the living room or kitchen. Windows, essential for natural light and ventilation, should also be thoughtfully located to avoid compromising personal privacy.

Safety: The bathroom should be a safe zone, addressing both physical safety and electrical hazards. Opt for waterproof and slip-resistant flooring to mitigate slipping accidents. Materials like calcium silicate boards, cement paint, and ceramic tiles are preferred for their moisture resistance. An efficient drainage system is vital to keep the space dry and easy to clean. Given the bathroom's humidity and heat, baths, electrical installations must adhere to the highest safety standards.

Cleanliness and Aesthetics: A bathroom should be a haven of cleanliness and visual appeal. Opt for a design that embraces simplicity, making it easier to maintain a clean and orderly space. Decorative touches and color schemes should aim for a balance between style and practicality, ensuring materials chosen are both attractive and straightforward to clean. This approach not only elevates the comfort of the user but also ensures the bathroom remains a pleasing retreat within the home.

Integrated and Transitional Living Room Interiors

In the quest to create fluid and versatile home environments, integrating spaces like studies and balconies with bedrooms or living rooms is a game-changer. These areas can either stand alone within the home or act as transitional spaces that bridge the gap between separate areas. Whether it's for solitary activities or socializing with guests, these integrated spaces redefine the traditional living room, offering a more cohesive and adaptive interior landscape.

Fig 3.25:Sanitary spaces design 2

Study Room

Multifunctionality

The study room wears many hats, serving not just as a quiet nook for reading and writing but also as a professional space for business discussions and client meetings. In homes where the vibe might clash with the casualness of a living room, the study offers a formal yet personal workspace. Tailoring the study to fit the family's needs can transform it into a dynamic area - for those with a penchant for the arts, it becomes a sanctuary for creativity, complete with spaces dedicated to painting and showcasing art.

Essential Design Principles

Quietness: The cornerstone of a productive study is its ability to foster focus through quietness. This can be achieved through a thoughtful layout and the right choice of materials. While open studies integrated into living spaces offer convenience, they may fall short on tranquility. In contrast, a closed study, ideally located away from the hustle and bustle of household activity, guarantees minimal noise. Employing soundproofing and acoustic materials is key to creating a peaceful environment conducive to concentration.

Comfort: Comfort in a study is not just about physical ease but also about creating an environment that minimizes stress and boosts productivity. With electronic devices being a staple, managing the heat they generate is crucial; this is where greenery and air conditioning come into play, maintaining a comfortable temperature range of 24°C to 28°C. Proper ventilation is equally important for air quality and preventing lethargy. Lighting, too, plays a pivotal role; it should be ample and strategically placed, with spotlights illuminating workstations and reading areas to ensure clarity and reduce eye strain.

Fig 3.26:Study room design

Fig 3.27:Open study room design

mirror the user's personality and lifestyle. Achieving this means designing a space that harmonizes workstations with areas for relaxation, reading, and multimedia enjoyment, all customized to the inhabitant's preferences. Incorporating elements like a cozy sofa and coffee table can create a snug corner for unwinding with a book or enjoying a leisurely tea break, adding a personal touch to the workspace.

By adhering to these principles, designing a study becomes an exercise in creating a space that not only meets functional needs but also enhances productivity and well-being.

Verandahs (Balconies)

Multi-Purpose Spaces

Balconies are much more than just an extension of living space; they're versatile areas where daily chores meet relaxation. Not only do they function as convenient spots for drying clothes, but in larger homes, they transform into personal gyms, tranquil retreats for yoga, or cozy nooks for soaking in views and gentle breezes.

Designing with Purpose

Balconies can be tailored to fit two main roles: practicality or leisure. Functional Balconies: These are your workhorses, ranging from 3m² to 8m², mainly focused on chores like laundry. To ensure they serve their purpose well, keeping them uncluttered and open to sunlight is key.

Leisure Balconies: Then there are those dedicated to relaxation and social vibes, designed as welcoming spaces for enjoying the scenery, hosting get-togethers, or simply unwinding. The abundance of natural light makes them perfect for a green touch, with potted plants and flowers elevating the space's look and feel. Additionally, incorporating elements that provide shade can transform your balcony into a serene, outdoor haven that connects you with nature right at home.

By aligning design with desired functionality, balconies can effectively blend utility with pleasure, making them invaluable assets to any residence.

Fig 3.28:Balcony design

Fig 3.29:Large balcony design

Types of Styles for Living Room Interiors

1. Overview of styles of living room interiors
2. Chinese style
3. New Chinese Style
4. Japanese style
5. European style
6. American Style
7. The Southeast Asian Style
8. Modernist Style
9. Industrial Retro Style
10. Eclectic Mix and Match Style

Chapter 4: Types of styles for living room interiors

4.1 Overview of styles of living room interiors

Principles of stylistic design

The living room's design melds diverse elements seamlessly. It's all about smart space planning that draws from a mix of styles, color palettes that resonate with the dwellers' moods and tastes, and the thoughtful use of lighting and plants to elevate the room's vibe, mirroring the beauty of nature outside.

Holistic

Interior design involves a strategic blend of various elements, where the choice of color, material, and craftsmanship in furniture and decor is tailored to specific styles. During the design process, these elements should interact seamlessly, avoiding a haphazard collection. It's crucial to carefully prioritize and arrange these components to forge a cohesive and harmonious whole. This approach ensures that the overall style of the home is unified, fostering a sense of cohesion that pulls everything together beautifully.

Purposefulness

Each room's interior design reflects the occupants' lifestyle and taste while embodying the designer's aesthetic and design philosophy. Therefore, the style designer maintains subjective independence and purpose, avoiding the wholesale replication of existing decorative trends. Instead, they use style types as a design tool, integrating materials and decorative elements to create unique visual forms and design outcomes tailored to each individual home.

Relevance

In the world of living room design and decor, economics mingle with social dynamics to shape trends. In a market-driven environment, decor firms, media outlets, and developers engage in a dance of influence, guided by a mix of regulations and mutual give-and-take. To avoid the trap of profit-chasing, style creation needs a collaborative approach. Open dialogue and checks and balances between authorities, organizations, and homeowners are vital, forging a network of relationships that guarantee style designs are not only appealing but responsibly executed.

4.2 Chinese style

Formation and Development of Style

pot of styles. As modern tech merges with socio-economic and cultural shifts, cross-cultural dialogue is booming. Interior designs echo national heritage and cultural nuances, capture the zeitgeist, and subtly reflect local religious sentiments.

For example, after China's economic reforms and open-door policy, a wave of foreign influences redefined public aesthetic preferences, steering interior design away from traditional Ming and Qing styles and elaborate decorations. This transformation embraced Western post-Industrial Revolution design elements, offering fresh perspectives on traditional Chinese aesthetics and evolving into a modern Chinese style that resonates with contemporary tastes. Likewise, historical exchanges have nudged many Chinese homes to adopt Western living practices, leading to a rich tapestry of decorative styles, ranging from European and American to Southeast Asian, Japanese, and Islamic.

As science and technology advance at breakneck speed, they're revolutionizing countless sectors, including how we enhance our living spaces for better quality of life. Take Xiaomi's smart home system – it's a prime example of how tech is being woven into the fabric of living room design. A well-rounded interior considers not just the occupants' lifestyles, personalities, and beliefs but also the broader social tapestry and technological landscape. This holistic strategy isn't just about functionality; it's about crafting living spaces that are as comfortable and healthy as they are stylish. The aim is a living room that doesn't just look good but feels good too.

Boasting a legacy over 5,000 years old, from the era of the Shang and Zhou dynasties, Chinese architecture has stood the test of time, carving out a unique niche in the world's design panorama. With each chapter of its storied past and cultural evolution, it has blossomed into the distinct and visually stunning New Chinese style – a style that weaves tradition with modernity, celebrated as a jewel in the crown of global architectural diversity.

Table 4.1 showcases the evolution of architectural shapes and furniture decorations shaped by China's rich cultural heritage over various eras.

Table 4.1: China's Cultural Legacy and Its Impact on Architectural Styles and Furniture Design

Era	Architectural Style	Furnishings	Cultural Influence
Shang Zhou (c. 1600-1046 BCE)	Monumental patriarchal temples and palaces, strategically placed on elevated sites	Essential household items: low-set beds and tables	Driven by religious practices and social stratification

Chapter 4: Types of styles for living room interiors

Qin Dynasty	Palatial complexes with functional zoning	Stately high platforms as symbols of imperial might	Structural hierarchy reflecting power, status, and identity
Han Dynasty (206 BCE-220 CE)	Development of advanced raised-beam structures	Ornate murals as prominent decor features	Influenced by Confucian and Taoist ideologies
Wei (220-265) and Jin (265-420)	Architectural diversity due to minority influences	Advent of portable furnishings like foldable beds and screens	Emphasis on harmonizing buildings with natural surroundings
Sui (581-618) and Tang (618-907)	Lavish palaces adorned with glazed tiles	Variety in furniture height; embellished with immortal and landscape motifs	Sheng Tang culture with a penchant for inclusivity and diversity
Five Dynasties	Dominance of private estates and pavilions	Landscape motif screens among staple furniture pieces	Retreat-seeking literati culture; burgeoning landscape art
Northern (960-1127) and Southern Song (1128-1279) Dynasties	Exquisite and intricate architectural designs	Integrated seating arrangements; prevalent use of decorative textiles	Rise of literary and artistic refinement within domestic spaces
Yuan Dynasty (1279-1368)	Central Asian architectural influences; colorful brickwork	Elevated tables; murals depicting landscapes, flora, fauna, and festive lanterns	Fusion of Han traditions with diverse ethnic practices
Ritual Sacrifices	Grandiose structures with defined hierarchy	Functional, unadorned furnishings	Manifestation of stringent social order; development of scholarly culture
Qing Dynasty	Emphasis on craftsmanship and detailed regulations	Practicality-oriented pieces; introduction of Western-influenced items	Adherence to social hierarchy; openness to emerging cultural ideas
Contemporary	Eclectic architectural influences; post-1949 Soviet impact, adoption of concrete	Mix of Eastern and Western furniture styles	Cross-cultural influences reshape design ideologies; modern technology fuels innovation

Fig 4.1:The Chinese style is showcased by incorporating traditional Chinese furniture, ink painting, bonsai, and other decorative elements. The design also incorporates traditional techniques such as borrowing scenery

50

Design Concept of Chinese Style

Incorporating traditional Chinese history and culture, the Chinese style emphasizes the principle of "*harmony between man and nature*." This design philosophy unifies the natural environment with the internal space, treating the interior as an integral part of the architectural context. It promotes a symbiotic relationship between the interior and exterior, infusing elements like natural light, wind, and air into the design blueprint.

The design of interior spaces necessitates a consideration for both the residential structure and its surroundings, ensuring an uninterrupted continuity. The interplay between individuals and their built environment is integral, as no element of Chinese style design exists in isolation. With its people-centered approach, Chinese style design seeks to manifest living spaces that align with the inhabitants' lifestyle and aesthetic sensibilities, while echoing traditional Chinese cultural philosophies and the quintessence of its cultural spaces.

Spatial design of Chinese style

The Chinese style, deeply ingrained in China's extensive historical and cultural legacy, has blossomed into a refined and sophisticated aesthetic, rich with profound and varied cultural underpinnings. It moves beyond the confines of specific dynastic influences, prioritizing the conservation and articulation of a spiritual essence and emotional depth.

In modern residential design, the integration of Chinese style has been tailored to complement contemporary living practices, ensuring its relevance and functionality for today's inhabitants, while still encapsulating the core of its cultural origins.

Spatial hierarchy

Traditional Chinese aesthetics and architectural space flow are anchored in a profound understanding of spatial hierarchy. Practices like winding paths, borrowed landscapes, and the strategic use of frames in classic gardens showcase this spatial planning philosophy. These techniques masterfully add depth and intrigue, steering clear of straight sightlines and predictable pathways.

Take the living room, for example, where elements such as partitioned windows, intricate lattices, screens, and moon gates serve to define different areas. These elements, harmonizing with the furniture's character, amplify the space's complexity and openness, reflecting the multi-layered elegance of Chinese interior design.

Layout symmetry

Chinese style planning and spatial arrangements often emphasize symmetry and balance to foster a sense of stability and elegance. This symmetry, however, is not about rigid duplication but rather about achieving a harmonious equilibrium. This is evident in the meticulous selection of color ratios and layouts that ensure visual coherence, as

To further enhance the overall harmony of the space, decorative details such as floral, avian, aquatic, and insect motifs can be integrated. These elements not only diversify local details but also imbue the space with a natural charm and intrigue.

Furniture ornaments in Chinese style

Chinese style design marries traditional cultural motifs with the demands of modern living, shedding outdated traditional furniture for forms that resonate with contemporary tastes and activities. This evolution streamlines intricate carvings and blends in Western design ideals that prioritize functionality.

The material palette is still rooted in natural wood, yet it transitions from the classic, heavy sandalwood and agarwood to lighter, more readily available woods such as walnut and beech. This shift modernizes the decorative approach while maintaining the classic red and black hues of Chinese furniture, now adapted to suit individual preferences for a space that's both stately and stylish. This modern yet respectful nod to heritage appeals strongly to middle-aged and older individuals.

The ornamentation of Chinese style furniture typically includes:

Ceiling

In traditional Chinese architecture, ceilings often feature wooden strips laid out in a square grid pattern. For contemporary living spaces embracing a Chinese aesthetic, ceiling designs can be simplified without losing their essence. A straightforward method includes a solid wood frame fitted with embedded lighting, which may be painted to match the overall interior theme, creating a cohesive and elegant atmosphere.

Doors and Windows

In the realm of Chinese-style interiors, doors and windows act as platforms for showcasing traditional designs, often realized through detailed latticework carved from solid wood. Beyond their decorative function, doors and windows also serve as spatial dividers, framing vistas and establishing a rhythmic flow that mirrors the continuity and balance of a scroll painting.

Furniture and Decor

Chinese style furnishings play a dual role, enhancing the space while also mirroring the cultural richness and social status of the occupants. For example, in a study, traditional calligraphy, paintings, plaques, scrolls, and bonsai are preferred over conventional decorative art, fostering an intellectual atmosphere and a distinctive cultural aesthetic. In the living room, ceramics, screens, and antique shelves are thoughtfully placed to highlight the residents' cultivated tastes and treasured collections. Additionally, arrangements featuring pine, plum, bamboo, and chrysanthemums are incorporated, adding greenery and deepening the room's symbolic layers.

Fig 4.2;The Chinese-style ceiling design retains a rectangular shape and incorporates a wooden texture, maintaining a cohesive and authentic look

Characteristics of Chinese Style Design

Residential Interior Design in Chinese Style

Merging Chinese style interiors with Western design sensibilities and cutting-edge technology culminates in a clean, strong, and unambiguous aesthetic. This harmonious blend produces a design that's not only straightforward but also packs a punch, showcasing a fresh take on classic Chinese motifs.

Utilization of Straight Line Decorations

Straight line decorations in Chinese style interiors reflect traditional values of subtlety and restraint, embodying a simple yet refined aesthetic. This design not only emphasizes the modern focus on functionality and practicality in furniture but also elevates the quality of life, closely aligning with current design trends.

Incorporation of Geometric Shapes

By simplifying traditional furniture styles through the use of geometric shapes, the essence of the design is captured, creating both sleek and eye-catching pieces. For example, assembling quadrilaterals to form a frame for a decorative landscape painting, displayed on a feature wall, not only updates traditional cultural motifs but also adds a unique Chinese elegance and charm to the room.

Merging warm lighting with natural sunlight and indoor yellow tones achieves a balanced atmosphere. This approach not only promotes a more relaxed pace of life but also encourages inhabitants to unwind and deeply appreciate the traditional cultural aesthetics.

Fig 4.3:He distinctive features of Chinese-style design are showcased, with an adept use of straight lines and geometric elements to create a visually appealing spatial layout. Additionally, warm lighting is employed to enhance the ambiance and create a cozy indoor atmosphere

Cultural Embodiment in Chinese Style

Exploring Tea Culture in Design

China's profound traditional culture has greatly shaped modern design, providing a rich lexicon and array of elements. Taoist principles such as "*harmony with nature*" and "*effortless action*," along with the use of white space in paintings and the sophistication of the tea ceremony, heavily influence Chinese design aesthetics. This book explores how tea culture, a cornerstone of Chinese artistry, impacts design.

The tea ceremony's evolution traces back to the sencha ritual, later refined during the Southern Song Dynasty. It rose to nationwide prominence during the Tang Dynasty, especially among the intellectual elite. For these connoisseurs, tea drinking transcended the act itself, reflecting life philosophies, artistic appreciation, and intersecting with the teachings of Confucianism, Buddhism, and Taoism. In China, tea art is seen as an expression of natural philosophy.

Creating a Tea Ceremony Atmosphere

The atmosphere of a tea ceremony is skillfully shaped by the design of the tea table and the choice of utensils. A typical arrangement includes five essential components: spatial design, mat selection, tea set combination, accessory choices, and tea snack pairings.

To enhance the living room layout, space planning should ideally connect with the natural surroundings, such as through full-length windows or balconies. This connection allows tea activities to blend with the outdoor views, creating a comfortable, leisurely, and inviting ambiance. The aesthetic tastes of the residents and the local living environment influence the design of the tea table, ensuring that the elements and primary colors harmonize to evoke a distinctly Chinese tea room style.

The tea set, central to the arrangement, often features warm, simple black pottery and purple sand, or fresh, elegant white porcelain and celadon. Different tea sets symbolize the varying moods associated with the tea ceremony.

4.3 New Chinese Style

Formation and Development of Style

China's embrace of reform and international ideas has sparked a cultural renaissance, blending Western motifs with post-modern sensibilities to redefine the nation's artistic expression. Designers are at the vanguard, merging age-old Chinese motifs with the latest Western design techniques and post-modern thought to forge an innovative Chinese style.

The esteemed architect Mr. Liang Sicheng identified four architectural streams: traditional Chinese, ancient Western, contemporary Western, and modern Chinese. He championed modern Chinese architecture as the zenith, symbolizing a seamless marriage of historic elegance and contemporary innovation.

The Emergence of the New Chinese Style

With social and economic growth fueling elevated lifestyles and home habits, there's a rising demand for quality living spaces that honor cultural heritage. The New Chinese style is at the forefront of this movement, an avant-garde design approach steeped in historical richness, architectural legacy, and aesthetic principles. It weaves together the threads of tradition with the innovation of modern technology and style, meeting the dual desires for comfort and cultural resonance. This fusion gives life to living spaces that not only serve contemporary needs but also radiate the distinct allure of China.

Differences between New Chinese and Chinese styles

Variations in Overall Layout and Material Selection

Traditional Chinese interiors, with their symmetry evocative of palace architecture, command a majestic aura. New Chinese design, however, tends toward the lighter, favoring asymmetrical layouts that embody simplicity and layering, yielding a more balanced, serene, and inviting

Material choice is another distinguishing factor. Traditional Chinese designs rely heavily on wood, often ornately carved with motifs like dragons and phoenixes, lending a sense of solemnity and grandeur. This technique, though striking, can be costly. In contrast, the New Chinese style broadens the material palette, embracing not only wood and stone but modern elements like glass and wallpaper.

Color Palette in Traditional and New Chinese Styles

Traditional Chinese interior design boasts an understated yet sophisticated palette, with red and black anchoring the scheme, complemented by muted, warm tones. Meanwhile, the New Chinese style breathes new life into the spectrum, employing wallpapers and glass tiles for dynamic wall and floor accents, and infusing bolder, more vibrant hues—crimson, gold, azure, and emerald—into its decorative repertoire.

Furnishing Shapes in Traditional and New Chinese Style

Traditional Chinese style is known for its elaborate and varied line work, with furnishings often showcasing detailed carvings that exude elegance and sophistication. On the flip side, the New Chinese style, under the influence of modern design principles, opts for a cleaner, more straightforward approach. It cherishes simplicity in layout, using clean lines and minimalist shapes to integrate traditional Chinese motifs, moving away from elaborate carvings towards a sleek, modern look that resonates with the younger crowd.

Materials in New Chinese Architecture

New Chinese architecture enriches spaces with cultural depth by seamlessly merging traditional materials with modern alternatives, paving the way for greater environmental sustainability and design efficiency.

Glass

Thanks to its brilliant ability to let light in while keeping noise out, glass has become a go-to for home partitions. Today's glass designs boast a variety of styles that not only serve a function but also add a touch of elegance, making them a key feature in the fresh, New Chinese style homes.

Wallpaper

Wallpaper, acclaimed for its vast selection of colors and patterns, offers a simple yet transformative solution for interiors, earning it widespread popularity. It presents an economical method to infuse interiors with a Chinese-style ambiance, appealing to those aiming for the New Chinese aesthetic without stretching their budget.

Antique Tiles

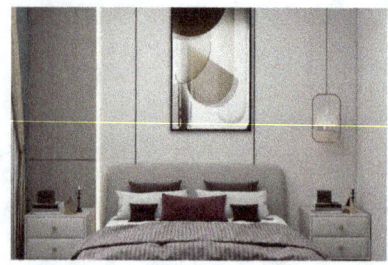

Fig 4.4:The use of linen brown and other coordinating fabrics in the new Chinese-style design helps create a space ambiance that is closer to the Zen-like essence of Chinese style

Known for their vibrant hues and textures, these glazed tiles provide a wider color range and superior stain resistance than their traditional counterparts, though their durability could be enhanced. Antique tiles are a beloved choice in New Chinese design, frequently adorning floors in kitchens, bathrooms, and balconies.

Traditional Materials in New Chinese Design

Fabrics in New Chinese decor serve as a gentle touch that eases the room's ambiance, with an array of choices from woven to three-dimensional textures. Where traditional styles parade peonies and lotuses in vibrant, lucky colors for prosperity and fortune, New Chinese design opts for subtlety—light and elegant tones with a nod to modernity through abstract patterns.

Marble's rich texture, enduring quality, and versatile hues have made it a go-to for decorative flair in flooring, partitions, and feature walls. Its use in interior design not only boosts the visual charm but also adds a touch of timeless elegance.

Wood, a linchpin in Chinese aesthetic heritage, continues to hold sway in New Chinese style, especially through the use of pear and sandalwood. In furniture, screens, and accent walls, wood is the medium of choice to evoke a tranquil, Zen-like atmosphere, while also bringing a traditional coziness and familiarity unrivaled by other materials.

Furniture in New Chinese Style4

The New Chinese furniture style breathes fresh life into traditional Chinese classics and culture, skillfully blending modern craftsmanship with contemporary aesthetics to create pieces that are vibrant, organic, and comfortable.

Form: This innovative style shatters the conventional furniture hierarchy, drawing from the Tang, Ming, and Qing dynasties yet distilling traditional elements into sleek geometric forms. This simplification not only preserves the style's inherent stability but also aligns it with contemporary lifestyles, yielding a lighter, more dynamic aesthetic.

Color: A transition from rosewood to revitalized walnut as the dominant material ushers in a palette of brighter hues, enriching the living room with an enhanced sense of elegance in the New Chinese style.

Chinese style and reducing its heaviness and opulence

In the realm of New Chinese furniture, the age-old mortise and tenon joinery stands firm, embodying strength and doubling as a contemporary design feature that injects both energy and a rhythmic nod to tradition into each piece. Design elements such as truncated legs, intricate framing, and structural posts are seamlessly woven in, serving dual purposes of utility and visual charm.

Color Usage in New Chinese Design

Color is pivotal in New Chinese design, serving to amplify spatial ambiance and grace with a serene, Zen-inspired palette. While classical Chinese culture favors deep, regal hues like red and dark brown, often

Fig 4.5:The new Chinese-style furniture elements still feature Chinese influences, but with a more simplified design in terms of shape and color compared to traditional Chinese furniture

accented with gold to denote status, Western palettes lean towards lively, unique warm colors offset by cooler shades to achieve a balanced atmosphere.

The New Chinese approach weaves Western color strategies with China's rich chromatic legacy, catering to contemporary tastes while respecting historical significance. It calibrates color schemes to resonate with different demographics:

For the Youth: Light, warm colors blend with inventive lighting to craft spaces that are cohesive yet echo traditional motifs.

For Mature Audiences: Deeper, reddish-brown shades prevail, utilizing nuances of light and shadow to create a grounded yet inviting environment, rich without excess.

Heritage Architectural Hues: Echoing ancient residences and Suzhou gardens, these set the primary design tones.

Time-Honored and Earthy Colors: Traditional colors form the base, enriched with natural tones that articulate the authentic charm of Chinese culture.

Beyond colors, New Chinese style marries modern aesthetics with time-honored art forms, enhancing traditional Chinese culture. The use of ornaments and symbols imbued with historical significance adds depth, with ornamentation falling into three distinct categories.

Ornamental Elements in New Chinese Style

In the New Chinese style, space dividers like traditional Chinese gates, porthole racks, and screens play a pivotal role, yet they're best utilized with restraint and simplicity to enrich the spatial experience without overwhelming it.

Traditional Ornaments: The essence of heritage lives on through the art of calligraphy, ink painting, scrolls, and the presence of antiques. Adding a layer of cultural depth, plants such as plum, orchid, bamboo, and chrysanthemum, revered in Chinese lore, weave historical significance into the decor.

Symbolic Patterns: Iconic imagery, including dragons, phoenixes, and clouds symbolizing good fortune, serve as vibrant carriers of Chinese tradition. Whether adorning background walls or acting as accent pieces, these symbols inject dynamism into the space.

In crafting spaces, the key lies in the judicious use of traditional motifs to preserve the New Chinese style's hallmark simplicity. Drawing inspiration from the compositional techniques of traditional painting and calligraphy, such as the strategic use of negative space and landscape-inspired layouts, can elevate the spatial ambiance. This approach not only refines the aesthetic but also uplifts the inhabitants' quality of life by creating serene, harmonious environments.

4.4 Japanese style

Formation and development of Japanese style

Origins of Japanese Style

Earlier discussions on Chinese style highlighted the Tang Dynasty's architectural interior design as a cornerstone. Japanese furniture has since embraced and safeguarded Tang heritage, blending it with their own cultural nuances and lifestyle practices to forge a distinct, all-encompassing Japanese aesthetic. For example, the Tang shift from kneeling to seated living spurred the development of low furniture, which resonates with Japanese living habits and compact living spaces. Japanese decorative motifs likewise echo Chinese brushwork and landscape art, yet are imbued with a distinctly Japanese essence.

Development of Modern Japanese Style

The infusion of Western lifestyles, with their comprehensive ergonomic designs and advancements in architectural and decorative crafts, has markedly influenced traditional Japanese design principles. This cross-cultural exchange has birthed the modern Japanese style, a fresh aesthetic that marries Western innovation with Japanese tradition. Despite the pervasive influence of the West, Japan's strong sense of national identity has anchored its core lifestyle choices. The prevailing design philosophy among residents and designers is one of blending the global with the local.

In practice, this philosophy materializes in living spaces that juxtapose modernity with tradition. Apartment interiors may showcase modern European-style designs and furnishings in common areas, while private spaces cherished by families and individuals retain quintessentially Japanese elements like tatami mats and sliding paper doors. This approach underscores a harmonious balance, celebrating both foreign innovation and the enduring spirit of Japanese tradition.

Land Privatization and Privacy in Japanese Design

In Japan's landscape of wholly private land, "*No Trespassing*" signs are a frequent fixture, spotlighting the value placed on clear boundaries and personal privacy. This cultural hallmark drives the demand for architectural designs that not only define but also defend one's private sanctuary.

Absence of Fences

In Japan, renowned for its strict adherence to law and order, traditional fences are frequently supplanted by hedges encircling buildings. This method not only delineates private from public spaces but also amplifies the greenery, creating a seamless and organic link between indoor and outdoor settings.

Parking Space Allocation in Japanese Homes

In Japan, despite high car ownership, subterranean garages are rare, hindered by limited land availability and precarious geological conditions. Consequently, parking solutions are ingeniously integrated at ground level within residential building complexes.

Dual Entrances in Japanese Homes

In Japan, homes typically feature two distinct entrances: a formal one for guests and a more utilitarian rear entrance, known as a katsudo, for family use. This setup prevents dirt from being tracked inside, keeping homes pristine. The katsudo, usually near the kitchen or bathroom, streamlines outdoor clean-up.

Stepped Entrance Design

A hallmark of Japanese homes is the genkan, or entrance area, which includes a shoe cupboard and a raised step, marking the transition from outdoor to indoor spaces. This not only facilitates shoe changing but also combats moisture and humidity, prevalent in Japan's maritime climate.

Earthquake-Readiness in Japanese Housing

Given Japan's susceptibility to earthquakes, seismic-resistant construction is paramount. Residential structures, often two to three stories tall, employ lightweight materials and feature rubberized supports at their bases for added stability. High-rises are rarer, as the need for stronger foundations and complex steelwork escalates costs.

Bathroom Zoning for Wet and Dry Areas

Fig 4.6:We have a Japanese-style residence

In Japanese homes, a clear division separates the toilet from the bath, creating two interconnected but standalone areas. This layout not only guarantees privacy but also streamlines bathroom use and simplifies maintenance, greatly elevating the living experience.

Japanese style design elements

Japanese Interior Design

Japanese design, rooted in Zen philosophy and tea ceremony traditions, values simplicity and harmony. In its spatial planning, it minimizes physical barriers to promote fluid movement, striving to "*create a room with spatial flow.*" This approach allows the aroma of tatami mats to infuse the home. Utilizing semi-transparent paper and natural wood tones, the design reduces spatial isolation and crafts a serene, Zen-inspired interior with clear, textured lines.

Design Elements of Japanese Style

Japanese interiors master the art of subtle lighting and soft partitions, often using shoji screens and curtains for gentle separation. Given the compact spaces and traditional sitting customs, furniture tends to have a low-profile design, featuring items like ground-level tables, beds, and cabinets. These pieces are usually made from natural woods—beech, birch, cypress, cedar, and pine—showcasing the timeless, nature-inspired ethos of Japanese design.

Fig 4.7: We have the essential element of tatami mats in traditional Japanese homes, which have been a prominent feature throughout history. They continue to be used today to create a sense of spaciousness in small living spaces and offer versatile functionality

Tatami Mats

Tatami mats, essential in Japanese decor, are often rectangular, adhering to a standard 2:1 aspect ratio. The typical size is 1800mm by 900mm, with common thicknesses of 35mm, 45mm, and 55mm—55mm being the preferred choice. These mats are best placed atop a well-constructed wooden subfloor, not directly on concrete.

When it comes to trim, choices include shades of blue, fuchsia, and turquoise. Blue trims are usually seen in public spaces, while fuchsia and turquoise are more personal, favored in homes. Made from natural materials like straw and rush, the trim features patterns ranging from zigzags to tic-tac-toe and balanced designs, adding a touch of artistry to the mat's edge.

Flooring

Flooring options with built-in lift tables fall into two categories: standard and designed. The standard models maintain a height range of 150-200mm. Designed floors, however, account for both the lift table's thickness and its height when collapsed.

For a flawless installation, these innovative floors require a solid foundation—starting with a keel and topped with fine planking or plywood. This ensures a smooth, even surface. Moreover, when embedding a lift table into the flooring, it's crucial to reserve a central opening for the lift mechanism, seamlessly blending functionality with design.

Painted Doors, Sky Pockets, and Floor Pockets

Painted doors, often chosen for closets and room entryways, typically stand at 1900mm tall and 800mm wide. While custom designs can push these dimensions to 2100mm in height and 930mm in width, it's essential to balance size with space.

For cleverly concealed storage, look to sky pockets above and floor pockets below closets, usually measuring 800mm by 400mm. Custom storage solutions should be mindful of their limits—no taller than 600mm or wider than 930mm.

Dividing spaces with style, partition doors and windows come into play, with the standard door size being 2000mm by 750mm. For those seeking taller doors, extensions above existing structures are possible, and custom sizes can reach up to 2200mm in height and 920mm in width. For a partition door, the window frame should boldly overlap the door's edge, and the mullions should stand straight and true. In tight spaces, or where existing windows challenge new additions, think about installing a fan-shaped partition window for both light and ornamentation.

Fig 4.8: We have the simple and elegant design of Japanese sliding doors, which are enriched with textures to serve both as space dividers and decorative elements

Niches and Daiten Tachi Columns

Niches, integral to traditional Japanese ceremonies, are often set within painted closets or beside doors. Custom-sized to fit their surroundings, they typically measure around 900mm and are illuminated with spotlights to create a solemn atmosphere.

embodying the essence of Japanese religious decor. Ideally positioned in niches or by painted doors, they enhance the sacred space. When spatial limitations arise, the emphasis shifts to capturing the spirit of tradition through decorative elements, rather than strict layout rules.

Walls and Flooring

Wall treatments typically fall into two categories: wallpaper and top paper. Wallpaper often boasts light hues with delicate dark patterns, whereas top paper leans towards a rich, dark wood grain appearance. Walls adorned with wooden beams and columns should be complemented with sleek wooden trim, creating sharp right angles devoid of ornate detailing.

When it comes to flooring, choices range from hard surfaces like bamboo, crafted from natural elements, to soft options such as foot and floor mats, which offer both comfort and aesthetic appeal.

Ceiling

1. For a spacious feel that draws the eye upward, outfit ceilings with dark-colored top slots. Dangle pendant lamps to infuse warmth, and keep everything else sleek for an elegant, modern vibe.
2. Embrace nature by incorporating horizontal wooden beams as a design element. Nestle Japanese lamps within these beams to marry simplicity with sophistication.
3. Emulate a classic Japanese aesthetic with wooden board ceilings that boast minimal embellishments, save for understated Japanese lamps, fostering a zen-like tranquility.

For lighting, select fixtures that blend function and style, such as bamboo lamps, sleek modern spotlights, or whimsical paper lanterns.
Ornaments

A rich assortment of ornaments graces these spaces, including iconic Japanese dolls, samurai figurines brandishing swords, traditional portraits of elegant women, fan art, and a hearth. To enrich the ambiance, antiques, kimonos, intricate embroidery, and a variety of Japanese flora are frequently incorporated into the decor.

Glass Windows

Traditional Japanese interiors often incorporate moon windows—either circular windows or round mirrors affixed to walls—to visually enlarge the space. These apertures are typically adorned with petite curtains or, for a more practical touch, blinds. If curtains are preferred, they are often crafted from antique, muted-tone fabrics, fostering a serene, luminous atmosphere.

Fig 4.9:We have the simple and elegant design of Japanese lighting fixtures, which are complemented by recessed and spotlights to provide ambient lighting in the space

4.5 European style

Formation and development

The Ancient Greek Epoch

At the heart of European culture lies the rich legacy of Ancient a civilization that thrived on the liberal and democratic ethos of its city-states. This cultural bedrock not only championed democratic ideals and scientific inquiry but also cultivated a unique relationship with the divine, marked by a blend of reverence and playful engagement.

The Greeks expressed their spirituality through an array of artistic endeavors — from poetry and painting to song and dance, all dedicated to the pantheon of gods. Among these artistic innovations, temple architecture stands out as a monumental achievement, setting the stage for European art and culture's ongoing odyssey. These architectural marvels, beyond their immediate religious and civic functions, laid the foundational stones of classical heritage, leaving an indelible mark on the trajectory of European cultural evolution.

The Ancient Roman Era

The towering achievements of Ancient Roman architecture didn't just rise from the ground — they were built on the artistic bedrock laid by the Greeks. The Romans took the scientific theories of their predecessors and fused them with a flair for functionality, venturing into uncharted architectural territories. Their creations stand today not only as artistic wonders but also as feats of engineering that have stood the test of time.
In stark contrast to the aesthetically-oriented Greeks, the Romans played a different tune, favoring grand scale, precise proportion, and utilitarian design. Both the silhouette and substance of Roman architecture cast long shadows over Europe, shaping the built environment for centuries to come and leaving a legacy that still captivates the modern imagination.

The Byzantine Era

Byzantine architecture, standing at the crossroads of ancient Greek and Roman traditions, took the classic elements of columns, vaults, and arches to new heights. It introduced the innovative sail vaults, which revolutionized interior spaces with a sense of openness and liberation. The Hagia Sophia's majestic central dome stands as a testament to this architectural leap, dazzling visitors with its grandeur and engineering marvel.

Driven by a deep religious fervor, Byzantine builders wove a tapestry of rich, harmonious colors and intricate, lavish decorations into their designs. The art of mosaics, in particular, emerged as a hallmark of Byzantine style, adding a layer of divine sparkle to the interiors. This era of architecture marries the structural innovations inherited from its predecessors with a unique aesthetic vision, creating spaces that are not only places of worship but also gateways to the heavens.

Medieval Western Europe

In the tapestry of Western European architecture, the medieval era unfolded with a measured grace, navigating through the Romanesque and Gothic periods with the 12th century marking a pivotal era of transition.

architectural landscape for an evolutionary leap.

Enter the Gothic era, a period that built upon the Romanesque groundwork but dared to reach for the skies. It introduced a symphony of architectural innovations: pointed arches sang of ambition, ribbed vaults echoed with complexity, while steep roofs, bell towers, and balustrades added rhythm to the skyline. The ensemble was enriched with clustered columns, intricate tracery, and stained glass windows that painted light into divine hues, all harmonized by the recurring motif of the pointed arch. The Notre Dame de Paris stands as a crowning achievement of this period, embodying the Gothic spirit in its purest form.

Together, these periods weave a narrative of architectural evolution in Medieval Western Europe, from the grounded solemnity of the Romanesque to the aspirational heights of the Gothic, capturing the essence of an era that looked to the past for inspiration and to the heavens for aspiration.

The Renaissance

The Renaissance, a beacon of cultural and architectural rebirth, illuminated a world eager for growth and prosperity. This era saw a resurgence of the classical column system, which became the backbone of a style that prized order, proportion, and meticulous composition in both facades and plans.

Renaissance architecture was distinguished by its dignified solemnity, substantial volume, and exquisite craftsmanship. The palette was rich, the details were intricate, and the surfaces were alive with artistry. Buildings were adorned with detailed paintings and carvings that brought human figures, flora and fauna, and tales from ancient Greek mythology to life, transforming structures into canvases of cultural narrative.

This period not only redefined architectural aesthetics but also set a new standard for the integration of art and structure, creating a legacy that continues to inspire awe and admiration.

The Baroque Period

Emerging from the structured elegance of the Renaissance, Baroque architecture danced into the spotlight with a flourish of drama and extravagance. This period broke free from classical constraints, embracing fluidity, diversity, and a theatrical contrast of lights and shadows that played across surfaces in a mesmerizing display.

Baroque buildings are a feast for the senses, adorned in lavish colors and materials that catch the eye and ignite the imagination. This style revels in romantic dynamism, with every curve, arch, and column designed to evoke a sense of movement and emotion. Exaggeration and opulence are not just elements but the very soul of Baroque architecture, making each structure a bold statement of creativity and grandeur.

In essence, the Baroque period redefined architectural expression, infusing structures with a life and vibrancy that continues to enchant and inspire.

Baroque, is the epitome of lightness and charm in 18th-century design. This style is best exemplified by garden mansions that stand as an antithesis to classicism's austerity and Baroque's heavy ornamentation. It embraces a whimsical, almost feminine grace with its delicate, refined aesthetics.

The furniture of the Rococo era is as much a work of art as it is a testament to comfort—slender in form, lightweight in presence, and meticulously crafted. Comfort isn't just a luxury; it's essential. Cherry wood often serves as the canvas for these pieces, with the color palette favoring pastel hues, soft golds, and blushing pinks that evoke a sense of playful elegance.

In Rococo, the whispers of nature are ever-present, with decorative motifs celebrating the outdoors—plants entwined in intricate patterns and bucolic scenes capturing the leisurely pleasures of hunting and fishing. Each design element invites a dance of sophistication and whimsy, making Rococo not just a style but a sensory experience.

The Neoclassical Period

The Neoclassical period heralded a revival of architectural rationality and solemnity, steering away from the ornate flourishes of previous styles. This era was characterized by a focus on creating lighter, more expansive interior spaces that echoed the clarity and balance of ancient Greek and Roman designs.

A shining example of this style is the Paris Pantheon, often simply called the Pantheon. This iconic structure embodies the Neoclassical ideals of grandeur and simplicity, with its vast, open interiors that invite contemplation and reverence. The Pantheon stands as a testament to the enduring appeal of classical proportions and the power of architecture to inspire awe through its sheer scale and thoughtful design.

In essence, the Neoclassical period reaffirmed the timeless beauty of classical architecture, blending it with a modern sensibility that continues to influence architectural design today.

Blending Tradition with Modernity: The Evolution of European Design

European interior design, drawing from the rich wellspring of ancient Greece and Rome, masterfully integrates the architectural heritage of Europe. This approach to design offers a full spectrum of aesthetic appeal, from the sweeping grace of spatial layouts to the fine craftsmanship of individual pieces of furniture and decor. The style presents more than ornate splendor—it weaves a tapestry of casual sophistication and enchanting romance.

Material selection and attention to detail in European design don't just happen by chance—they're the result of a designer's keen aesthetic judgment and hands-on expertise.

The modern iteration of European style holds true to the core values of honesty, nobility, and elegance that are hallmarks of its classical antecedents. Yet, it strips away any hint of superfluous complexity or overwhelming luxury. Today's European design marries functional pragmatism with advanced materials, ensuring that each piece is as practical as it is stylish. This fusion results in designs that are both

Fig 4.10: We observe the intricate and elaborate details of European-style wall decor, furniture, and ornamental flowers

elegance in a way that resonates with contemporary life.

Carved Elegance: The Hallmarks of European Furniture

European furniture stands out for its solid build, ornate detailing, and lively hues, all of which transport a touch of aristocracy and grace into any space. A signature trait of such pieces is their elaborate carving—expert hands etching nature-inspired motifs that do more than just catch the eye; they significantly elevate the worth of each item.

These hand-carved treasures are masterpieces of proportion and symmetry, ensuring every swirl, leaf, and figure is placed with precision. The color schemes are nothing short of a romantic reverie, with deep and vivid tones that bring the furniture's story to life.

European furnishings are characterized by their diverse designs and smooth, curvaceous silhouettes, often showcasing the quintessential curved "animal feet" on the legs—a nod to a bygone era of opulence. The contours flow seamlessly, proving that in the world of European design, elegance lies in the details.

Solid Woods and Luxe Fabrics: The Cornerstones of European Furniture

European furniture is synonymous with the robust charm of solid woods like beech, teak, oak, and cherry. These woods provide a symphony of hues yet maintain an elegant uniformity, steering clear of jarring contrasts. This dedication to a harmonious color scheme speaks to the quintessential European flair for subtlety and sophistication.

When it comes to upholstery, only the finest of fabrics make the cut. Velvets that are soft to the touch, supple leathers, and silk brocades rich with history are often adorned with intricate embroidery, adding a layer of aristocratic allure.

Hardware is not just functional; it's part of the furniture's soul. Utilizing bronze, gold, and silver, European furniture pieces don't just sit in a room; they elevate its entire ambiance to one of pure opulence.

With changing times, the domestic decor landscape has seen a shift towards classical elegance. Today, interior aficionados and homeowners alike are revisiting classical furniture forms, infusing them into modern spaces. The contemporary market offers an array of wooden furniture that smartly blends solid wood with engineered panels, striking a balance between aesthetic and practicality. This innovation addresses the traditional shortcomings of all-solid-wood pieces like warping and cracking. Yet, make no mistake, the allure of all-solid-wood with its unparalleled craftsmanship, tactile pleasure, and heirloom quality remains unmatched.

Cultivating Elegance: Furniture and Decor in Harmony

To create a space steeped in Western sophistication and grandeur, selection and arrangement of furniture are key. For homes echoing a European motif, it's wise to choose compact, functional, and modern furnishings to keep the space tidy and open.

The interplay of furniture with the room's layout and choice of accents is paramount. Each piece should complement the interior's contributing to a cohesive and vintage European flair. Introducing a variety of materials in both furniture and decor can infuse the room with depth, while the overall scheme should resonate with the wall and floor finishes for visual symmetry. Every item tells a story; some add a touch of majesty and gravitas, others whisper tales of romance and subtle grace.

As design sensibilities evolve, the European style remains afloat by preserving classical roots yet simplifying ornate details. This balance of tradition with modern tastes has refreshed the aesthetic, making it more relatable and fitting for contemporary lifestyles.

Textiles: The Heartbeat of European Interior Design

In the world of interior design, textiles are more than just fabric—they're the architects of ambiance. European-style textiles set themselves apart with their deep, vivid colors, a result of sophisticated color weaving and precise printing techniques. The favored materials range from the soft embrace of cotton and silk to the lush opulence of satin and velvet, all chosen for their ability to blend comfort with luxury.

But European textiles don't stop at just color and material. They're a playground for intricate detailing, where lace, embroidery, and jacquard techniques bring depth and narrative to each piece. Whether woven into the fabric of satin and cotton or standing alone, these embellishments are the brushstrokes that paint a picture of European romance and elegance.

These fabrics do more than furnish a room; they envelop it in a texture and richness that captivates, transforming ordinary spaces into realms of lavish comfort and sophisticated charm.

European Wallpaper: From Lavish Elegance to Understated Chic

Wallpaper is to a room what a canvas is to a painting, and European-style wallpaper comes in two distinct styles, each with its own flair for transforming spaces.

The first style is a nod to the grandeur of Europe's past, with wallpapers that boast vibrant and varied patterns. These designs are a tapestry of foliage and florals, meticulously arranged in different sizes to weave a rich tapestry of order and intricacy, breathing opulence and sophistication into any room.

In contrast, the second style is the epitome of 'less is more.' It favors a natural and polished look, with a lean towards the minimalistic. Think clean lines, understated stripes, subtle florals, and geometric forms. This approach isn't just about patterns; it's about creating a seamless flow with the furniture and decor, resulting in a tranquil, cohesive space that speaks volumes with its simplicity.

Whether it's commanding attention with elaborate designs or creating a serene retreat with muted patterns, European-style wallpapers have the power to set the mood and lift the spirit of a space.

Drapes and Rugs: Weaving Elegance into Every Room

Curtains are the chameleons of interior decor, offering a transformative power with their array of fabrics and designs that add they present an array of fold densities that invite the eye to dance across their surfaces, injecting life and interest into the space.

On the floor, carpets lay a foundation of understated elegance. Usually thick, always grounding, they broaden the room's palette with patterns and hues that speak in soft tones, creating a harmony that resonates with the soul. These so-called secondary accessories might fly under the radar, but they're paramount in achieving an aesthetic equilibrium. They do more than comfort the feet or dress a window—they bring a polished grace to the living space, tying together the loose ends of decor with a silent, yet powerful, flourish.

Elevating Spaces: The Art of European Floor Decor

In the realm of European-style interiors, the devil is truly in the details, especially when it comes to flooring. Solid wood floors take center stage, boasting wavy lines and intricate parquet patterns that are particularly adept at making smaller spaces feel intimate and inviting. For larger expanses seeking to convey a sense of grandeur, stone tiles become the material of choice, laying down a foundation of timeless elegance.

When it comes to carpets, the rule of thumb is to embrace subtlety. Selecting shades that harmonize with, yet stand out from, the furniture and walls creates a distinguished look that's both cohesive and captivating. The patterns on these carpets are a visual feast—featuring figures, flora and fauna, landscapes, and geometric shapes—all designed to weave together a tapestry of classical elegance that's synonymous with European design.

In this way, floor decorations do more than merely cover a surface; they set the stage for a room's entire aesthetic, anchoring the space in a tradition of refined beauty.

Crafting Elegance: The Art of Furniture Decor

Sofa sets are often dressed in the luxurious textures of velvet or satin, which are then jazzed up with decorative pillows to amplify the visual opulence and harmony of the room. Bedding, on the other hand, is crafted with a touch of sophistication, sometimes adorned with delicate tulle, intricate lace, and elegant shaped pendants. These embellishments sometimes mirror the fabrics of the room's furnishings and curtains, weaving a seamless tapestry of style that ties the space together.

Fig 4.11:The fabric is complemented by the carpet and plush toys, serving as elements in space arrangement. The intricate patterns of the fabric create a sense of depth and complexity

In essence, furniture decoration is not just about comfort; it's a canvas for expressing the refined taste and attention to detail that defines a truly elegant living space.

Illuminating Elegance: European-Style Lighting

European-style lighting, a masterful dance of light and shadow, not only casts a romantic glow but also doubles as a statement piece of art. The spotlight often falls on ornate fixtures like wrought iron and crystal chandeliers. Their curved lines, diverse shapes, and premium materials harmonize to brighten interiors with both light and liveliness. Crystal lamps stand out for their clear, subtle design, elevating the play of light

Fig 4.12:The living room lighting features a variety of options, including water feature pendant lights, strip lights, and lampshades

stage. This focused illumination is perfect for crafting a romantic and sophisticated atmosphere, offering a warm, inviting glow that tempers the grandeur typical of European decor. It highlights the personal touch, making spaces not just majestic, but truly homey.

Embellishing Elegance: The Art of European Ornamentation

In European-style interiors, the focus is on the lavish use of curves and detailed craftsmanship, whether it's the grand scale of furniture and walls or the intricate details of decorative pieces. Nature is the muse here, with patterns inspired by stems, buds, vines, and other graceful natural forms woven throughout the decor, breathing life and diversity into the space. Wall, railing, and furniture patterns range from free-flowing and organic to meticulously detailed, with countless fine elements arranged with precision. Master craftsmanship shines through in techniques like painting the edges of carved elements. Common motifs include landscapes, figures, plants, and animals.

Decorations are not just accents; they are expressive elements, often crafted from materials like copper, silver, ceramics, and glass. Decorative paintings play a pivotal role, their metal frames not only reflecting the owner's refined and noble artistic taste but also echoing the opulence of the space. These elements work in harmony to create an ambiance that's both elegant and atmospheric, emphasizing a sense of refined luxury.

Fig 4.13:European-style decorations often include floral arrangements, glass products, copper picture frames, and mirrored glass, which add a diverse range of items to small spaces

4.6 American Style

Formation and Development of American Style

Colonial Period

The genesis of American design can be traced back to the colonial period spanning from 1607 to 1733. As European influences permeated the American continent, they catalyzed a fusion with Native American decorative arts, which began to emerge and gain traction. This cultural amalgamation significantly influenced both furniture and architectural styles, with a penchant for ornate decorations. Venetian windows and wooden floors became hallmarks of the era. Middle-class furniture often mirrored Tudor and Jacobean styles, exemplified by the evolution of the Windsor chair into the late Jacobean chair, characterized by elongated forms, scrollwork, and upholstery. Lamps and decorations frequently featured various types of silver, and Chinese blue-and-white porcelain also found its way into interior decor, adding a touch of exotic elegance.

The Federal Period: A Classical Revival in American Design (1780-1830)

The Federal Period, spanning 1780 to 1830, marked a pivotal shift in American design towards classical elegance. Architectural features began to echo the timeless beauty of Greek revival styles, inspired by the works of renowned architects such as Palladio and Serlio. This era, influenced by sweeping societal changes, saw the interiors of the elite adorned with sophisticated decorations. Spaces were characterized by lush red velvet with a simplified yet intricately detailed decorative approach. This period underscored a refined aesthetic that married simplicity with grandeur, reflecting the nation's aspirations and cultural evolution.

The Victorian Era: A Bold Departure in Design (1837-1901)

The Victorian Period, stretching from 1837 to 1901 and named after Queen Victoria, marked a bold reimagining of classical artistic values amidst the dawn of new creative visions. This epoch stood in defiance of the Industrial Revolution's mechanical aesthetics, ushering in an era of design and decoration characterized by complexity and vivacity. Interiors burst with bold hues such as red and gold, signaling a departure from the subdued tones of previous periods. Furniture often took on an imposing presence, oversized and crafted with an exuberance of materials. Wood paneling was applied liberally, contributing to the lavishly textured and richly adorned spaces that typified Victorian design sensibilities. This period underscored a return to opulence, with a keen eye for intricate details and a penchant for the dramatic.

The American West Period: Embracing Rustic Simplicity (18th Century)

In the 18th century, pioneers in the American West cultivated a warm and unpretentious decorative style known as American country. This aesthetic seamlessly blends local decorative elements with the surrounding natural landscape, utilizing indigenous materials to create rustic interiors. Spaces are characterized by sturdy wooden ceilings, floors, and windows, enhanced by log-toned furniture. Earthy hues like brown, green, and yellow are thoughtfully integrated, mirroring the natural environment. American country style often features vintage furniture and ornaments, including wooden pieces deliberately marked with signs of wear, adding a touch of nostalgia. Nature-inspired design elements, such as animal prints and floral motifs, are commonplace. The fireplace stands as a pivotal feature, not only providing warmth but also serving as a central gathering point that enhances the cozy and harmonious ambiance of the home. This period celebrates a return to the basics, emphasizing simplicity and a deep connection with nature.

American Design: A Tapestry of Style and Function

American style in design is a melting pot, reflecting the rich history and diverse culture of the United States. Today's American aesthetic, a blend of modernist clarity and rustic charm, prioritizes both simplicity and function with a focus on comfort and approachability. It weaves in natural elements and cultural touches, striking a balance between practical use and visual pleasure. The modern American look is all about creating spaces that feel tailor-made, lived-in, and welcoming—a true reflection of the American spirit.

American Furniture: A Rustic Elegance

American furniture design champions a rustic, natural charm,

Fig 4.14:American furniture featuring modern materials

These materials frequently undergo a "*distressed*" process, intentionally displaying marks from fire, files, or hammers to infuse a sense of historical depth and to resonate with a profound nostalgia and connection to nature. This approach not only enhances the aesthetic appeal but also fosters a sense of timelessness and authenticity in the space.

The design further integrates a mix of materials—leather, fabric, marble, glass, and metal—ensuring that each piece not only serves practical purposes but also embodies the multicultural amalgamation that defines American society and its aesthetic inclinations. This blend of textures and materials creates a harmonious balance, offering both functionality and a visual narrative that speaks to the diverse and dynamic nature of American culture.

Fireplaces: A Timeless American Icon

Fireplaces have been a cornerstone of American design since ancient times, reaching a zenith in the 18th century. The abundance of timber in the Americas led to early colonial fireplaces being framed in wood, lined with clay and plaster for fireproofing, and embellished with sturdy, raised wire frames, transforming them into focal points of interior design.

As society and the economy evolved by the late 18th century, fireplace designs became more sophisticated. The hearths in halls diminished in size, and decorative elements such as mountain flowers, plants, and sculptures depicting scenes from Aesop's fables were integrated. Above the fireplace, oil paintings and other artworks replaced the more utilitarian objects like shotguns that were prevalent in earlier American periods. This shift not only enhanced the aesthetic appeal of the fireplaces but also reflected the growing cultural sophistication of the era.

Siding: The Skin of American Style

Siding has played a significant role in shaping American architectural aesthetics, marrying modern culture with cutting-edge technology. Not only does it improve a building's curb appeal, but it also boosts thermal stability and sound insulation, harmonizing a space's look and feel with its practical utility. Siding comes in various sizes and shapes, typically falling into four primary categories:

The Art of Wall Panels: Crafting Cohesive Spaces

Wall panels, complete with molding, crown moldings, baseboards, and feature walls, seamlessly integrate hidden doors to maintain a consistent design flow. These elements often employ symmetrical arrangements, instilling a sense of balance and wholeness in a room. Tailored to the resident's taste and design requirements, these panels can feature classical motifs, Roman columns, and other stylistic choices that contribute to a rich visual tapestry. True to the American aesthetic, these panels lean towards understated elegance, often opting for monochromatic schemes that resonate with contemporary sensibilities.

walls and columns, marries functionality with style in American homes. This design choice employs materials like tiles, marble, wood, and paint not only to shield walls from moisture and wear but also to provide a decorative touch that's a cinch to maintain. In crafting wainscoting, heights usually span from 3 to 6 feet, hitting the sweet spot at roughly 4 feet for both aesthetic appeal and practical coverage.

4.7 The Southeast Asian Style

Evolution and Characteristics

The Southeast Asian style, born in a region often called "*the land of a thousand islands,*" has evolved at the crossroads of tectonic plates, where most countries boast extensive, jagged coastlines hugging the Indian Ocean. The geographical position, paired with the natural and climatic diversity of the area, has paved the way for a rich tapestry of cultural evolution and diversity. History has seen these countries as melting pots, where colonial influences have interwoven with the region's indigenous Oriental traditions to create a distinctive style. The prevalence of Buddhism across these lands means that a Buddha statue is a common sight in homes, serving not just as a spiritual emblem for peace and protection but also as a focal point of interior decor.

Defining the Southeast Asian Style

Characteristics

The Southeast Asian style is defined by its emphasis on plush furnishings and meticulous attention to detail, utilizing contrasts and a blend of various elements to create a visually stunning effect. This approach results in a distinctive cultural signature that marries serenity and sophistication with a laid-back and leisurely lifestyle, reflecting a refined cultural palate in home interiors.

Incorporating logs and other natural materials, the interior design is further enriched by the lustrous glow of golden silk fabrics, all complemented by the warmth of soft lighting, culminating in an ambiance that is both opulent and peaceful.

With Buddhism deeply rooted in Southeast Asian culture, its influence extends to color schemes as well. The use of deep, rich hues, reminiscent of the religion's ceremonial colors, dominates interior design, setting the stage for an environment that is both exotic and grounded.

Design Points

Southeast Asia, a tropical region rich in resources, is renowned for its use of natural materials and handcrafted items in home design. This style reflects the vibrant, passionate, and natural characteristics of tropical rainforests, focusing on simple, clean lines in furniture rather than ornate details. The outcome is a sense of rustic authenticity and natural charm in the furnishings. Globally popular, especially in regions with similar climates, the Southeast Asian style is particularly appealing.

This style's robust, rustic decor is ideally suited for larger residential

Fig 4.15:Siding structure names also influenced by European textures

Fig 4.16:American siding Overall more inclined to the shape of simple, light color

Fig 4.17:Warm colors dominate the overall style of Southeast Asia, and religious colors are created through steps, window views, and niches

spaces, typically those exceeding 120 square meters.

Decorative elements in the Southeast Asian style blend Buddhist cultural influences with Thai classical traditions, fostering a profound Zen-like atmosphere. Local materials such as solid wood and rattan are employed to accentuate the design's primitive, natural essence.

In spacious homes, darker hues are predominantly used for expansive areas like walls and flooring, while lighter shades are reserved for decorative accessories and accents. Adding vibrant curtains can complete the aesthetic. In smaller homes, light colors can be used to enhance the softness of the interior furnishings.

Tropical broad-leaved plants are a staple in Southeast Asian style. For homes with ample space, incorporating an indoor pool with lotus flowers can create a refreshing and natural ambiance.

Elements of Southeast Asian Style Interior Design:

Soft Furnishings

The Southeast Asian approach to soft furnishings marries extravagance with simplicity, displaying a broad spectrum of styles. This eclectic mix fully captures the spirit of Southeast Asian design. Here, traditional furniture pieces are significantly inspired by Western aesthetics, featuring elegant curves, brass details, and sophisticated carvings.

Jewelry

Southeast Asian jewelry, often infused with striking exotic and religious motifs, has the power to transform a room with just a single piece. Take, for example, metalwork in the form of copper rosette lamps or hand-hammered copper pendant lights; these items are more than mere light sources—they're statement pieces. The region's tableware, frequently adorned in hues of light brown and emerald green, boasts intricate patterns reminiscent of ice cracks, a hallmark of Southeast Asian design. These rich cultural accents lend a sacred and exotic allure to any interior space.

Materials

The essence of Southeast Asian home decor lies in its commitment to natural materials. From the rattan of Indonesia to the river water hyacinths of Malaysia, and extending to seaweed and other aquatic plants, this style celebrates the beauty of nature. Trinkets, often made from coconut shells, corn kernels, and banana peels, retain their natural hues and textures, bringing an organic touch to any space. Among these are grass baskets, Indonesian rattan mats, and bamboo-woven lanterns. This fusion of earthy materials like raw rattan and wood, alongside soft fabrics, creates an inviting natural ambiance that's both serene and vibrant.

Color

daring hues bring a sense of energy to strategic spots within the room.

Thai silk, with its lustrous spectrum, is a cornerstone of this design ethos. It combats any potential for a monochromatic space to feel flat or constrictive. Draping Thai silk curtains or placing a swath near the bed introduces an effortless opulence to the room.

Vibrant yellows, deep greens, and rich reds are favorites for fabric-based decor, such as the lively array of Thai pillows that can infuse any space with life.

Purple, gold, and red are the go-to shades for that authentic Southeast Asian vibe, though they shine brightest when used sparingly as accent notes.

White serves as the harmonizing force, providing a visual breather that ties the bold color story together in unity.

Fig 4.18: Southeast Asia as a whole color into the original wood color, but at the same time will use green, yellow, red to embellish, enhance the space exotic style

Fabric

Southeast Asian interiors are renowned for their vibrant decorative fabrics, which include pillows and tablecloths, adding a splash of color and character to any space. These textiles range from the subtle elegance of off-white Vietnamese hemp to the bold brilliance of Thai silk and Indonesian satin, as well as the intricate patterns of Indian embroidery. These rich and diverse fabrics not only disrupt monotony but also infuse the room with a dynamic and spirited ambiance.

4.8 Modernist Style

Formation of the Modernist Style

The birth of the modernist style can be traced back to the influential Bauhaus School and its visionary founder, W. Gropius. He championed the idea that architecture is in perpetual flux, shaped by evolving ideas and technological advances. A proponent of the belief that the modern age should be reflected in its architectural forms, Gropius called for the use of novel imagery and a clear display of modern construction techniques.

At its core, modernist design is grounded in simplicity, shedding the shackles of the past to embrace minimalism and prioritize function and spatial efficiency. This approach seeks to revolutionize aesthetics through fresh material pairings and color schemes that depart from classical norms. Geometric lines and the incorporation of new-age materials like glass, metal, plastic, and engineered wood are hallmarks of modernism, symbolizing its forward-thinking ethos.

Modernist Design: Material Innovations and Applications

Materials

In the realm of modernist design, materials play a pivotal role, with natural elements such as stone, wood, and brick serving as the bedrock. Unlike traditional architecture, modernism highlights the interplay between these materials, employing cutting-edge techniques and modernist design embraces the use of contemporary materials like metal, paint, glass, and synthetic substances, which are integrated to create a distinct aesthetic that stands apart from the past.

Laminate Flooring

Laminate flooring, encompassing both laminate and solid wood laminate varieties, boasts a broader spectrum of colors and patterns than its traditional wood counterparts. This array of choices has cemented its status as a favored option for those looking to infuse modernity into their home decor.

Stainless Steel

Stainless steel commands attention as a decorative element, celebrated for its distinctive texture and robust durability. It shines, quite literally, with a reflective surface that mirrors and melds with the hues around it, casting dramatic glints and shadows under the light. This play of brilliance dovetails with the modern style's focus on inventive and pioneering design, adding a touch of sleek sophistication to any space.

Glass

Glass, celebrated for its sheer transparency and adaptability, elevates the aesthetic appeal of interior spaces with its pristine clarity. Whether it's frosted, clear, or mirrored, glass injects decorative flair and broadens the spectrum of spatial designs. It plays a pivotal role in modern decor, showcasing the style's fluidity and innovation through varying degrees of transformation and light play, making interiors not just seen but truly experienced.

Marble

Marble reigns as a premier choice for modern home decor, gracing floors, accent walls in living rooms, and kitchen and bathroom countertops alike. With a vast palette of varieties at one's disposal, the art lies in selecting marble that harmonizes with the home's aesthetic, tying together the threads of design. The secret to sophisticated interior decor often rests on the discerning choice of marble, making it the linchpin of luxury and style.

Furniture

Modern minimalist furniture champions function without forgoing style, boasting sleek, no-frills silhouettes. It's the play of bold color contrasts and the use of contemporary materials like tempered glass and stainless steel that create a space that's both on the cutting edge and inviting. To balance the sharp simplicity of minimalist designs, soft touches like plush fabric cushions are key—they add a cozy warmth, softening the interior and creating a welcoming contrast to the streamlined aesthetic.

Decoration

Today's homeowners hold art in high regard, with decorative

Fig 4.19: Modernist style furniture: Metal elements such as stainless steel are used in industrial construction and also in the design of bedroom furniture

becoming a go-to decor element. These pieces showcase abstract shapes and compelling visuals that meld effortlessly with modern furnishings, setting the stage for a striking and cohesive look. This blend of art and design not only adds character to living spaces but also amplifies the joy and delight experienced by those who call it home.

Lamps

Lamps, the quintessential modern decor staple, have undergone a transformation far beyond traditional styles, thanks to technological leaps. Today, they're available in a wide array of personalized shapes and materials, including metal, glass, and ceramics. When it comes to choosing lamps, you have options: they can either meld with the room's aesthetic or stand out as statement pieces. Whether through bold contrasts or the use of distinct materials, they can spotlight specific areas, adding depth and character to any space.

Backdrop

The accent wall stands as a cornerstone of contemporary design, breathing life into focal areas such as the TV space, behind the sofa, the bedroom, or the entryway. Creative options like textured wallpaper, ceramic tiles, or marble provide a canvas for personal flair, while adornments like vintage finds, statement clocks, or sculptures add a touch of sophistication. These touches do more than just please the eye—they resonate with the homeowner's quest for artistry and an elevated lifestyle.

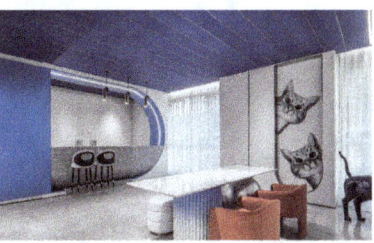

Fig 4.20:Modernist Background Wall Design: While using decorative paintings, (some background walls with higher reflectivity are used to enhance the vertical depth of the space

Modernist Color Design

In the realm of minimalist interiors, color choice is key to elevating the space. The deliberate employment of vivid, high-purity colors like emerald green, sapphire blue, pure red, and sunny yellow is a signature of modernist style. The function of the space dictates color application, swinging from monochromatic simplicity to bold, contrasting hues. The timeless trio of black, white, and gray, popular among the younger crowd, injects a sleek sophistication. Shades of gray, in particular, introduce a subtle complexity, polishing the space with an air of understated elegance.

Living Room

The living room, a sanctuary of simplicity, embraces the virtues of brightness and openness, often opting for airy hues such as white, soft beige, and gentle blue. The classic dance of black, white, and gray adds a layer of depth and harmony, crafting an environment that feels both expansive and freeing.

Dining Room

Today's dining rooms often blend seamlessly with the living room, preserving a consistent design aesthetic. Designers favor natural wood tones and angular dining tables, paired with contemporary art and illuminating fixtures. The result is a dining environment that strikes a balance between simplicity and clarity, all while exuding a subtle touch of romance.

Bedroom

The bedroom is crafted for utmost comfort and simplicity, featuring low-profile furniture that complements modern living, ensuring the space stays tidy and clutter-free. The color palette is cohesive and unified, with subtle shifts in color, light, and intensity, creating an environment that is tranquil, cozy, and peaceful.

4.9 Industrial Retro Style

Style Formation

The Industrial Retro Style emerged from the late 19th to early 20th century, a period marked by the rapid expansion of the industrial revolution. This era laid the foundation for what is often termed "*technological aesthetics*" or "*commercial aesthetics*," characterized by sharp lines, robust connections, and sturdy construction.

Revolutionizing Industrial Aesthetics

Industrial style redefines these aesthetics, with cement mortar—a key material—playing a crucial role in crafting the sleek, sanded walls and floors that epitomize the mechanical elegance of the early industrial age. The principles of Mies van der Rohe, such as "*Function comes first*" and "*Less is more*," embody functionalism within this style. His focus on utility and simplicity, as demonstrated by the German Pavilion at the Barcelona World Expo, highlights the potential of modern materials like steel and concrete in architectural design.

Evolution of Industrial Styles

The 1960s heralded the rise of what was then known as the high-tech or heavy technology industrial style. This design philosophy embraced "*machine aesthetics*" and seamlessly integrated cutting-edge technologies into the fabric of architecture and interior design. High-tech design schools favored materials like glass, metal mesh, and metal components for structural elements such as beams, floors, and stairways, often leaving these materials exposed to reveal the beauty of the infrastructure. Such design choices celebrated the raw, unpolished look of structural frameworks, air ducts, and cables – elements that became hallmarks of industrial aesthetics. To add visual punch, bold colors like red, green, yellow, and blue punctuated the design, offering dramatic contrast in piping or as vibrant accents.

At its core, the industrial style is about distilling and amplifying the technical components of modern design to symbolize new aesthetic values and meanings. Designers of this era sought to counter the predominant, warmer tones of Scandinavian modernism with a cool, masculine vibe that conveyed a sense of edge and sophistication. This approach not only challenged the status quo but also carried forward the principles of modernism, with its openness, industrialization, and technological flair. The industrial style gained momentum through a quest for perfectionism in architectural functionality and a yearning for the nostalgia of modern life.

As the 20th century drew to a close, China experienced a wave of architectural renovations that repurposed industrial buildings. This movement spawned artist studios and cultural epicenters, like those along Shanghai's Suzhou River, the Tank Warehouse at the Sichuan Academy of Fine Arts, the Art Filling Station in Beijing, and the iconic 798 Art District. These locales are distinguished by industrial-style edifices that artfully blend Chinese cultural elements, marking a unique evolution of this retro aesthetic.

Design Elements and Stylistic Application

The industrial style boasts a rich array of design elements. Historically, it merged with minimalism, as seen in the Moussou residence with its roof supported by exposed open-mesh frames and walls of glass and solid panels. Over time, blending 'industrial technology' with 'artistic flair' has eased the style's initial starkness and coldness. Designers have invigorated the style with bold experimentation and innovation, rendering it more dynamic and human-focused.

Smallpox

Industrial style sprang from the imaginative reuse of old factories and warehouses, which explains its signature raw ceilings, complete with beams, columns, and pipes, left untouched. The no-frills treatment often includes leaving concrete ceilings bare, with just a coat of paint in white, black, gray, or any chosen hue. Exposed pipes frequently get a similar splash of color, seamlessly integrating with the overall palette.

Walls

A key feature of the industrial style is its deliberate embrace of bare walls, showcasing exposed brick or raw concrete, and at times, even adding artificial aging to create a sense of history and character. This aesthetic prefers walls with a rough texture, employing materials like cultured stone, red brick, cement, cement board, mosaic tiles, distressed paint, and coarse wooden panels for a touch of decoration.

Floor

Flooring, beyond its functional purpose, plays a crucial role in shaping the atmosphere and style of an interior. In industrial design, flooring materials often include antique tiles, aged floor paint, and distressed wood. Antique bricks are popular, particularly those with muted colors and a weathered texture, like rust-imitation bricks. Aged floor paint, a specialty product, imparts a weathered look when applied over concrete. For wood flooring, choose gray or dark tones with visibly aged textures to enhance the industrial vibe.

Furniture

Metal furniture is a staple of the industrial style, symbolizing durability and a tribute to modern industry. The No. 14 chair, designed by Michael Thonet in 1859 using steam-bent wood technology, exemplifies this with its sleek silhouette, absence of armrests, and a curved backrest made from a single piece of bent wood. Although metal dominates in industrial design, its cold texture can render spaces stark if overused. Integrating metal with wood, however, harmonizes the aesthetic, infusing warmth while preserving the rugged character of the style.

Lamps

The arrival of electricity marked a turning point in human productivity and everyday living, fueling swift industrial expansion. British engineer Joseph Swan and American inventor Thomas Edison played pivotal roles in the invention and widespread adoption of the incandescent light bulb. Industrial-style lighting often showcases metal fixtures that sport a patina or signs of wear, complete with signature metal shades.

Fabric

Industrial style stands out for its mechanical, utilitarian, and bold aesthetic, sharply contrasting with the softness and warmth of textiles. Ornate European curtains, floral rustic bedding, and pillows often seem at odds with this style. To blend these divergent elements seamlessly, finding common ground that unites their distinct characters is crucial.

Curtains

Curtains are vital in any living space, used to modulate light, minimize UV exposure, and maintain privacy, thus amplifying indoor comfort. Echoing the steam era, the industrial style embraces period-associated features like prominent metal accents. To accentuate this style, opt for curtains with a metallic luster, such as those with a silvery silk finish. In industrial settings, furniture arrangements remain versatile, with curtains playing a subdued role. Sheer white gauze curtains are a popular pick; they gently filter light and views, softening the outdoor landscape to enhance spatial perception while effortlessly complementing the interior. Blinds, with their contemporary flair and consistent horizontal lines, mesh with industrial themes. Their slats can be adjusted for precise sunlight filtering, creating patterned light play in the room. Solid, unembellished curtains are the go-to, spotlighting minimalism and practicality, with hues that tie together the space's overall scheme.

Bedding

Industrial style bedding focuses on practicality, often omitting traditional elements like bed skirts and spreads. Common materials include cotton, linen, or silk with a metallic sheen, sometimes paired with a thick woven blanket or faux fur. The color palette is typically monochromatic and muted, though accented with occasional vibrant

Cushions in industrial decor should be straightforward, favoring square or rectangular shapes. Neutral tones dominate, with the occasional bright, saturated cushion adding contrast. Fabrics range from cotton and linen to metallic weaves and leather, often featuring a distressed or weathered look. Popular patterns include numerals, letters, geometric forms, and architectural motifs.

Carpets

In industrial style interiors, carpets are frequently used, similar to other design trends, typically in seating areas or by bedsides. Carpet hues are usually muted, with materials ranging from cotton or linen braids to sleek modern designs or traditional Persian patterns.

Decorative accents might feature numbers or letters made from iron, aluminum, or other metals; ironwork relics like vintage machine components; and an array of decorative paintings, ideally abstract black and white pieces, alphabets, or abstract motifs. These can be showcased on walls, shelves, or bookshelves, or casually propped against a wall on the floor or a side table.

Wall art or graffiti on chalkboard paint is also prevalent in industrial wall decor. Mechanical models, such as classic car replicas, steam forklift models, or biplane models, can effectively bolster the industrial vibe.

Transportation items like heavy motorcycles or bicycles double as both decorative elements and functional storage solutions. Bicycles can be displayed directly on the floor or mounted on walls.

Artifacts from the industrial era, including retro fans, old radios, dial telephones, and mechanical typewriters, contribute to the ambiance. Books are another essential decorative element in industrial style, either stacked on the floor or arranged on a large metal bookshelf.

Industrial Retro Style Color Scheme

Achieving the industrial style hinges on the color scheme. This design ethos, marked by a raw, gritty, and unique vibe, leans heavily on neutral hues.

Key tones include black, white, and grays. Black adds depth and tranquility, white brings elegance, and grays underscore the industrial vibe. Industrial spaces often showcase large swaths of these cool tones, with exposed brick walls adding a vintage feel and a textural contrast to smooth, painted surfaces. The shadows and light play between bricks offer a distinct visual compared to regular walls.

Natural shades like brick red, cement gray, and wood tones are also staples. This style celebrates the inherent beauty of materials—be it the warmth of brick, the starkness of cement, or the patina of metal. A red brick wall, for example, exudes simplicity, warmth, and vibrancy, especially when complemented by white, gray, and brick red, adding life and highlighting the wall's inherent appeal.

Introduce vibrant accent colors to break up the cool dominance. Since industrial interiors mainly feature cool shades, they can sometimes feel visually cold. Pops of saturated colors like red or yellow can warm up the space.

The interplay between color and material texture is vital; colors can instance, polished metals can make colors pop, while brick or cement might soften them.

Lighting plays a crucial role in how colors are perceived in a room. Warm lighting can infuse the space with cozy hues, softening the industrial style's often cold, stark ambiance. The golden glow of incandescent bulbs or the vivid brightness of neon lights are perfect for brightening and adding energy to the space.

4.10 Eclectic Mix and Match Style

Formation and development of free mixing styles

The term 'mash-up' originates from the practice of combining different ideas and theories somewhat mechanically and haphazardly. However, the mix-and-match style is a subjective, freestyle fusion that embraces personal taste and current fads. As society and culture have rapidly changed over the centuries, 'mash-up' has emerged as a contemporary trend, influencing various facets of life and industry.

This eclectic mix-and-match approach breaks away from the original, rigid structures and concepts found in many areas today, promoting a freer and more open mindset. 'Mash-up' goes beyond the physical, including 'mix and match' trends in fashion, music, and architecture, and even extends to abstract concepts like 'mixed emotions' and 'mixed culture.' Its adaptability is what defines the 'mash-up' approach.

Recently, the mix-and-match style has gained traction in living room interiors, reflecting a desire for innovative aesthetics aligned with personal taste. This style allows individuals to blend a wide range of styles and formal expressions into their living spaces, posing a creative challenge for designers amidst the complexities of contemporary society and culture.

A key tactic in mix-and-match design is the daring use of material finishes and color in furnishings. Designers may introduce bold colors such as red, blue, and yellow within a single space, forging sharp contrasts. The art lies in applying these colors thoughtfully and systematically, ensuring they harmoniously coexist to enhance spatial depth and modern appeal.

In the age of swift global information exchange, architecture and interior design have grown more diverse and interconnected. When building or decorating a home, inspiration can be drawn from both ancient and modern, Eastern and Western sources, resulting in a 'cross-era mix and match.' This less tradition-bound style employs a wide array of methods, but a closer look reveals an underlying order within its seeming randomness, the principle of 'order within disorder.' This is the crux of the mix-and-match method, where designers artfully combine elements to forge uniquely captivating works.

Rules for mixing and matching free mixing styles

The mix and match design philosophy unlocks a treasure trove of possibilities for tailoring unique styles. It's not simply about piling up various elements; it's about a thoughtful orchestration where each piece contributes to a harmonious ensemble. Whether marrying Eastern and Western aesthetics or weaving together the old with the new, both architectural and interior designs should pivot around a core design theme. From there, nuances and decorative flourishes can be woven in, provided they augment without overpowering the primary motif. The balance. Three Golden Rules of Mix and Match:

Color

In the mix and match style, there are no hard and fast rules for decorating. The main objective is to enrich the spatial depth of the home, enliven the surroundings, and foster a cozy, people-focused, and comfortable environment. Colors in this style can vary from muted, subtle grays to vivid, bold tones. However, when pairing contrasting colors such as red with green, yellow with purple, or blue with orange, it's essential to thoughtfully balance the proportions of each color's presence. Too much symmetry in the distribution of these contrasts can result in a visually jarring effect, detracting from the intended warmth and comfort of the living space.

Fig 4.21:General Rules for Free Mix and Match: Combining Different Element Languages to Form an Organic Whole

Matching of elements

The mix and match approach in design, much like a stream of eloquent prose, adopts a 'seemingly scattered yet intrinsically unified' strategy. Celebrated for its eclectic array of elements and their seemingly impulsive arrangement, this style demands a discerning eye for detail. In interior decor, every aspect—from the placement of trinkets to the balance of components within a room—warrants the designer's meticulous attention. The aim is to craft a space where each decorative piece seamlessly converses with the rest.

To hit the sweet spot in element utilization, the golden ratio—an ideal proportion of roughly 3 to 7—is often employed. An overabundance of items can clutter the focus and lead to excess, while too sparse an arrangement can leave the space feeling incomplete. Striking this balance is the cornerstone of forging a space that's both visually harmonious and compelling.

Materials

In the realm of mix and match decor, the palette of materials is extraordinarily varied, featuring traditional staples like bamboo, wood, and stone alongside contemporary options such as glass, metal, and porcelain. These materials no longer confine the style; rather, they open up avenues for merging diverse aesthetics.

While metal and glass are often used in moderation, primarily as elegant accents like lamp fixtures or picture frame trimmings, they lend a touch of refinement. In contrast, more substantial materials like wood and stone can dominate the design, bolstering the space's sense of permanence and stability.

Fig 4.22:Free mix and match of hair elements, size and shape are very flexible, and the placement and organization process need to conform to aesthetic logic

Three Key Characteristics of Furniture for Mix and Match:

Contrasting Styles: Furniture pieces with markedly different shapes, materials, and colors can be strategically placed in smaller rooms to foster visual contrast, enhancing the interior's richness and deepening the sense of space.

Harmonized Colors: Furniture with similar styles and forms but distinct colors can bind a space without overpowering it, making them perfect for expansive living areas where a unified feel is sought.

Exceptional Craftsmanship: Well-crafted, unique furniture items, celebrated for their design, are universally captivating and can be seamlessly integrated into any setting, elevating the overall aesthetic with their distinctive charm.

Program for Living Spaces

1. Overall Process of Living Spaces Design
2. Graphic Presentation in Living Spaces Design

Chapter 5: Program for Living Spaces Design

5.1 Overall Process of Living Spaces Design

Experienced interior designers carve out their own design workflows, while newcomers must get to grips with the design process's methodology. For beginners, grasping the overall workflow is a non-negotiable first step.

Living spaces design is a niche within the expansive realm of interior design, which itself is a facet of architectural design. The overarching aim is to fashion living spaces that are secure, user-friendly, and visually captivating. This is the beating heart of the endeavor. The process is a delicate balancing act, taking into account the architectural setting, the client's unique tastes, the spatial puzzle, functional limitations, furniture choreography, and even the potential integration of artificial intelligence in tomorrow's homes.

Positioning of Living Spaces Design

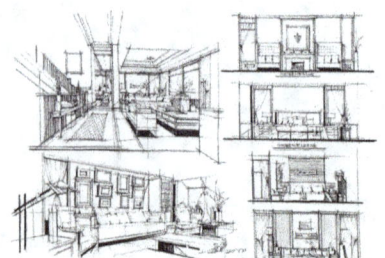

Fig 5.1:Fountain pen effect

The heart of living spaces design beats for creating personalized spaces that match individual lifestyles and routines. Unlike its public counterpart, this niche zeroes in on personal preferences. Kicking off the design journey demands a deep dive into a mix of straightforward elements like the setting's natural vibes, location, architectural style, and nuanced factors including the socio-economic backdrop, political climate, and local traditions.

Nailing the design's direction is key to landing the vision. Without a thorough analysis, all-encompassing consideration, and layered thinking, the foundation would be shaky. Designers need to become wizards with graphic tools during the positioning phase, translating the dance of flow lines, space layout, and functionality into clear visual language. This pivotal moment shifts gears from the abstract to the tangible, lighting the spark for design evolution and hands-on work.

Conceptual Planning Stage of Living Spaces Design

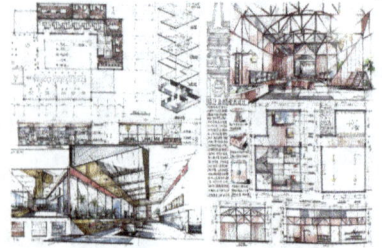

Fig 5.2:Interior design renderings and floor plans

Design concepts are fundamental cognitive constructs that bridge sensory perception and rational thought, reflecting self-awareness and underpinning conceptual reasoning. In China's GB/T15237.1-2000 standard, a concept is defined as a distinctive fusion of features that constitutes a unit of knowledge. Similarly, Germany's industry standard 2342 describes a concept as an abstract mental unit that encapsulates the shared traits of objects.

In the realm of residential interior design, the conceptual phase is marked by a thorough deliberation that marries design direction with goals to forge design concepts. This stage harnesses both deductive and inductive reasoning to craft the final concept.

Designers must adeptly employ graphic symbols to deconstruct and reformulate their ideas during this phase. Utilizing visual language not only fuels inspiration but also identifies design challenges, encouraging open-ended thinking and the pursuit of novel avenues. The interplay between sensory and logical faculties can ignite innovation through the varied expressions of this language.

While concepts begin as abstractions, they require material representation through the designer's hand. Realization occurs via spatial layouts, sketches, and a methodical cycle of comparison, refinement, and reorganization. A consistent application of visual language throughout the creative process enables designers to achieve optimal conceptual solutions.

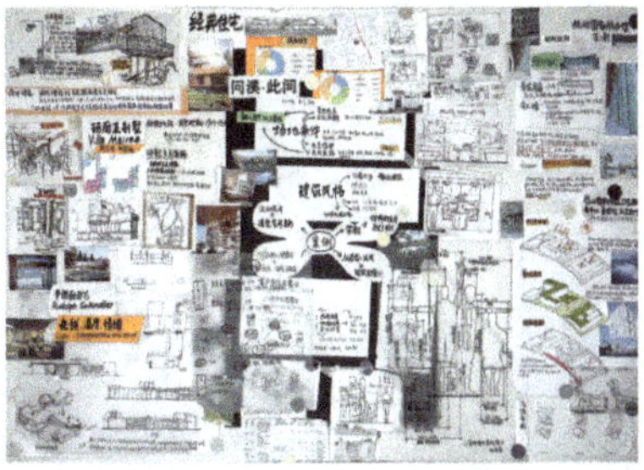

Fig 5.3:Design concept analysis ideas collage

Design Development Stage of Living Spaces Design

The design development stage is a critical phase in residential interior design, bridging initial concepts with the creation of detailed, actionable construction plans. This stage unfolds through three key phases: preliminary design, detailed design, and construction drawings. The culmination of the construction drawing phase signifies the near completion of the design process.

This phase is about bringing design ideas to life through precise architectural drawings. Modern design software enables designers to produce these drawings more efficiently and realistically than ever before, marking a significant leap from traditional hand-drawing methods. This technological advancement allows for greater focus on refining design concepts.

The success of design development is pivotal for the accurate realization of design concepts. It acts as the medium through which design ideas are communicated, with the quality of construction drawings directly affecting the precision of the build. Proper planning during this stage is essential to prevent frequent revisions later on, which could derail the project. Budget considerations also play a vital role in design development. Although detailed budgeting typically starts during the construction drawing phase, budget constraints are often a priority for homeowners. Designers must navigate these financial considerations early on, ensuring that even the most innovative designs remain within reach and do not become unfeasible due to cost constraints.

5.2 Graphic Presentation in Living Spaces Design

Living spaces design focuses on intimate, small-scale spaces tailored to individual households and their inhabitants. Novice designers often grapple with the constraints of limited living areas. To effectively convey these spaces, it's crucial to depict the spatial and temporal dimensions of homeowners' lives through design drawings, which requires designers to master graphic presentation skills. While drawing proficiency isn't equivalent to design expertise, it serves as a concrete demonstration of design proficiency.

Design schemes employ various graphic presentation techniques. Freehand drawing, or "*hand sketching*," is the first method. The second is computer-aided design (CAD), known as "*computer rendering*,"

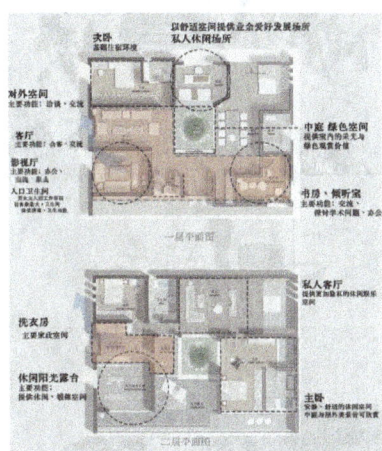

Fig 5.4:Spatial functional zoning map

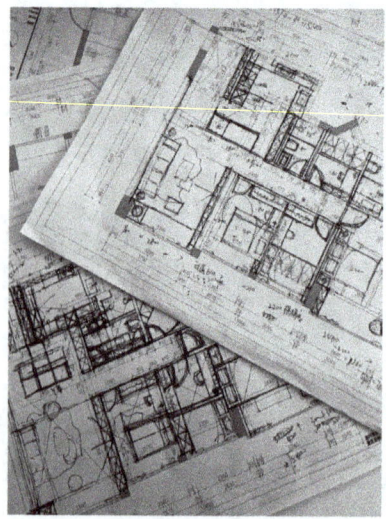

Fig 5.5: Hand-drawn floor plan

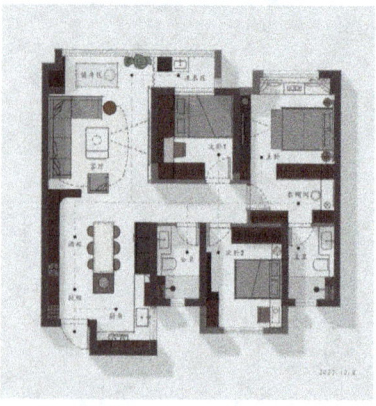

Fig 5.6: Interior floor plan layout ipad hand drawn

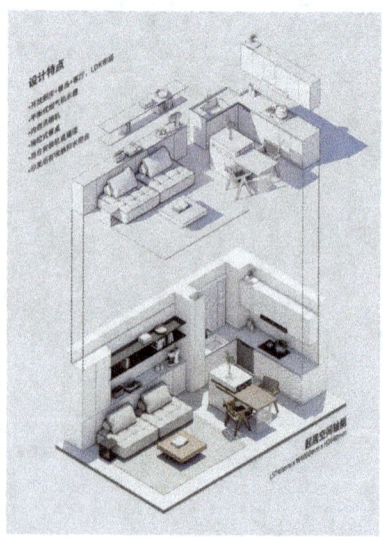

Fig 5.7: Sampling of living space

is widely used for its ease of modification and rapid drawing generation. Lastly, physical models are utilized, often seen in real estate displays. CAD is particularly popular due to its efficiency and enhanced visual effects. Common representations include floor plans, elevations, perspective renderings, and the emerging 360° panoramic VR experiences. Animated videos also showcase design effects. As we enter the 5G era, presentation methods will evolve, and AI may increasingly handle design representation tasks. Notably, both traditional hand sketching and advanced intelligent design are essential skills for designers. However, there's a growing trend of AI taking over tasks related to construction drawings.

Significance of Sketching the Floor Plan in Living Spaces Design

Sketching is a cornerstone in the creation of residential interior layouts, thanks to its casual and insightful nature. Many designers find that working with sketches fosters a deeper conceptualization of design solutions, emphasizing functionality over aesthetics. Floor plans, in particular, are instrumental for conveying the comprehensive design system and are a practical type of drawing. Given that residential interiors mirror the inhabitants' lifestyles, designers must skillfully balance various elements such as interior form, functional placement, decorative styles, furniture layout, and equipment systems to achieve harmony within the space. This process involves sketching numerous iterations of floor plans, undergoing several rounds of refinement, before moving on to the formal design development stage.

Expression of Living Spaces Design

The articulation of living spaces design effects within residential spaces showcases a designer's aesthetic flair. As the floor plan takes shape, the focus pivots to spatial arrangement and the visualization of design impacts. Crafting an effective design rendering goes beyond artistic depiction; it demands a strategic approach to the design narrative.

Key considerations for the design concept should include spatial geometry (be it angular or curved), the treatment of transitional areas at intersections, space optimization, resolution of inactive zones and movement conflicts, fidelity to design style and presentation, congruence of interior themes with spatial contour, functional lighting solutions, infusion of contemporary elements, and the creation of a cohesive and captivating style. Addressing these elements with diligence during the rendering phase sets the stage for a more streamlined development of construction drawings, a topic for further discussion.

In the living spaces design phase, designers should embrace expansive thinking, shatter preconceived notions, and sidestep cognitive confines. Each sketch, rooted in a distinct design idea, should open doors to further creative exploration.

With spatial designs set, the precise communication of visual information becomes paramount. Designers must recognize that living spaces design is underpinned by architectural principles, demanding an accurate portrayal of the design's essence. It's not simply an exercise in aesthetics but must account for practical considerations such as fire

Implementation and Construction Procedures of Living Spaces Design

1. Implementation Process of Interior Design in Living Spaces Design
2. Construction of Living Spaces Design

Chapter 6: Implementation and Construction Procedures of Living Spaces Design

6.1 Implementation Process of Interior Design in Living Spaces Design

Living spaces design is a meticulous process that demands systematic coordination across multiple departments. Designers must collaborate with a diverse array of stakeholders, including clients, construction crews, supervisory teams, material suppliers, and furniture vendors, to ensure the seamless execution of their design visions. Success hinges on client endorsement and the construction team's cooperation.

Designers function as maestros, skillfully managing demands and resources throughout the intricate implementation journey. Central to their coordination efforts are the client's attributes. The project sponsor's cultural heritage, financial status, perspective, and imagination profoundly shape the designer's creative direction. The client's social standing, educational background, and personal qualities, as well as those of their family, significantly influence the design trajectory. Effective client communication is often the linchpin of a design project's success. Furthermore, it's essential to assess the social context, architectural space, construction methods, and favored decorative styles.

Preparation of Design Assignment

To avoid pitfalls during the intricate design and construction phases, it's imperative to define and concur on the final design output with the client at the project's start. When the designer's vision isn't in sync with the client's, clear communication is key to harvesting valuable insights. The designer should record this feedback, which not only steers their creative compass but also pinpoints exact design parameters agreed with the client. Crafting this design brief guarantees that the design specs anchor the designer's work, sharpening the design journey and warding off shifts from the intended course due to diverse influences.

Design Research

With the design brief in place, the designer's next step is to undertake comprehensive preliminary design research, which profoundly shapes the concepts and solutions crafted during the design journey. This research encompasses a detailed analysis of the design subject and an exploration of design elements.

The analysis of the design subject seeks the optimal strategy to fulfill the brief's stipulations, laying a critical groundwork for conceptual

Chapter 6: Implementation and Construction Procedures of Living Spaces Design

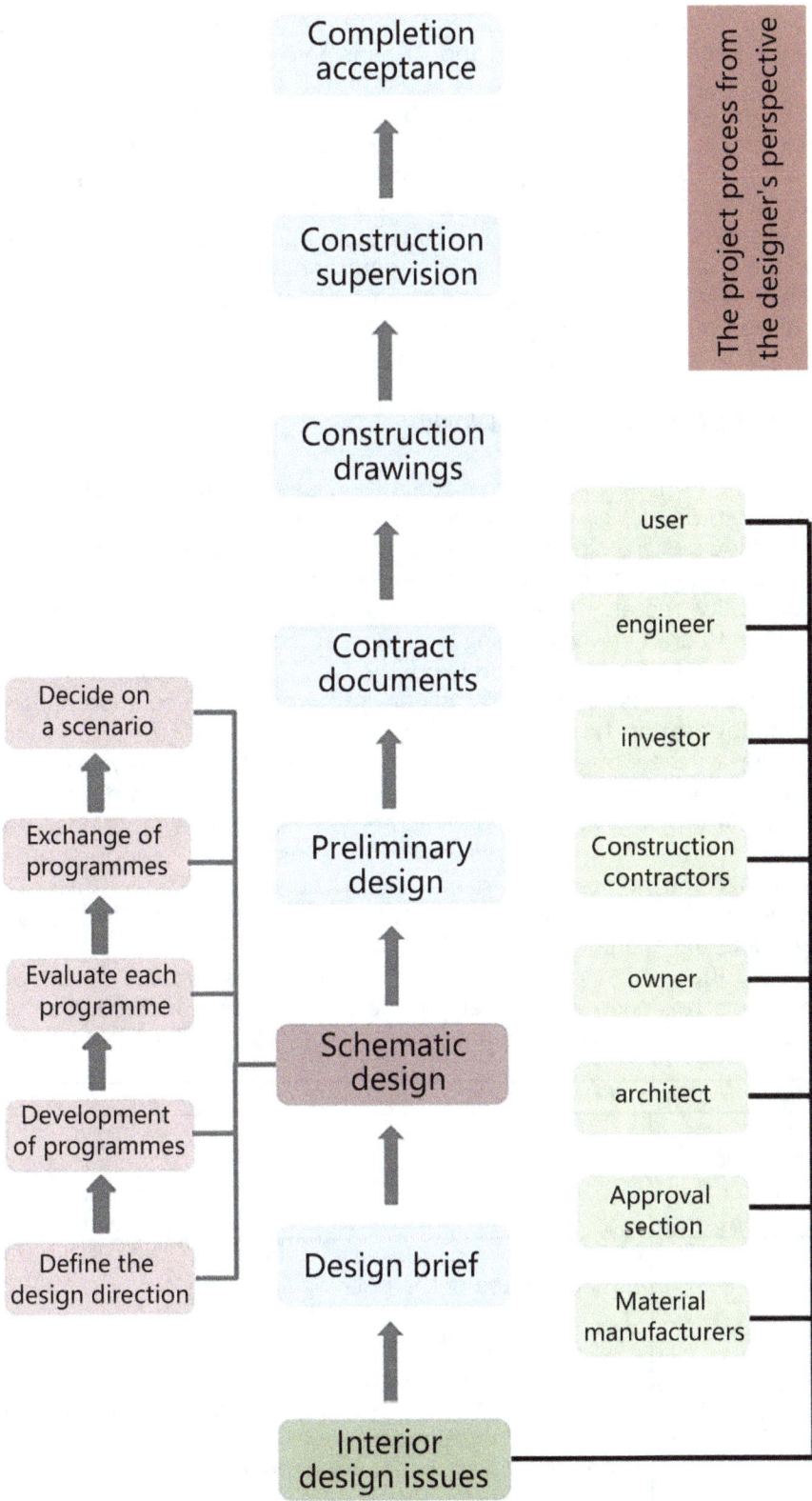

Example diagram of Living Spaces Design

client's functional needs for the space, 2) reflecting on the client's and their family's professional and cultural contexts, 3) assessing the client's financial constraints, and 4) considering the client's aesthetic inclinations.

Investigating design elements includes: 1) examining outcomes from similar projects, 2) reviewing pertinent domestic and international literature, 3) factoring in environmental surroundings, and 4) gathering data via site surveys of the living spaces design space.

These tasks demand meticulous attention, especially for novice designers, as they are pivotal for understanding in residential interior design. Even seasoned designers may find it challenging to fully grasp all design nuances, highlighting the necessity for rigorous analysis and research in the preliminary design phase.

Coordination of Design Work

Moving from comprehensive preliminary design efforts, we step into the conceptual design stage, a continuation from the prior chapter. Here, we employ design thinking to articulate the full scope of the residential interior design project. We weave together elements like spatial functionality, material selection, construction methodologies, and style definition to craft an overarching blueprint for the living space.

With the design blueprint in hand, the focus shifts towards seamless collaboration across various disciplines. In the design articulation phase, this collaboration largely pertains to refining blueprints. Yet, as we transition to executing the design, understanding the interplay between design elements and construction realities becomes paramount. No matter the project's scale, disparities between initial design visions and on-site conditions are almost inevitable. This scenario underscores the designer's pivotal role in managing the project, ensuring tight coordination and communication with the construction and installation crews, and the client.

Adapting design plans to accommodate construction needs or confirming the construction fidelity to design intentions underscores the importance of effective coordination.

Interior design of the professional system and coordination points		
Professional system	Coordination points	The type of work that is coordinated with it
Building systems	1.Functional requirements of the living spaces space of the building (involving the size of the space, the spatial sequence and the organization of the flow of people, etc.) 2.Correction and improvement of spatial shape. 3.The creation of spatial atmosphere and artistic conception. 4.Overall harmony with the architectural art style.	building

Structural systems	1.The utilization of exposed structural components in the interior wall and ceiling. 2.The relationship between the ceiling elevation and the structural elevation (net height of the equipment floor) 3.The way in which the indoor hanging objects and structural components are fixed . 4.The possibility analysis of the load-bearing structure at the wall opening.	structure
Lighting system	1.The relationship between ceiling design and lamp layout and illumination requirements. 2.The relationship between interior wall design and lamp layout and lighting mode. 3.Interior wall design and distribution box layout. 4.Interior ground design and lamp foot arrangement.	electric
Air conditioning system	1.Ceiling design and the layout of the air conditioning air outlet. 2.The interior wall design and the layout of the air conditioning return outlet. 3.The relationship between the indoor furnishings and all kinds of independent air conditioning equipment. 4.The relationship between the decoration design of the entrance and the layout of the cold air curtain equipment.	Equipment (HVAC)
heating system	1.Interior wall design and layout of plumbing equipment. 2.Ceiling design and heating system layout. 3.Entrance decoration design and hot air curtain layout.	Equipment (HVAC)
Water supply and drainage system	1.Toilet design and layout and selection of various sanitary ware. 2.Indoor fountain waterfall design and circulating water system setting.	Equipment water supply (drainage)

Fire protection system	1.Ceiling design and smoke alarm arrangement. 2.Ceiling design and arrangement of sprinkler heads and water curtains. 3.The relationship between the interior wall design and the layout of the fire hydrant box. 4.The selection and arrangement of the portable fire extinguisher that plays the role of decorative components.	Equipment water supply (drainage)
Transportation system	1.Interior wall design and elevator door openings. 2. Interior ground and wall design and automatic trail decoration treatment. 3.Interior wall design and decoration treatment of escalators. 4.Decoration treatment of barrier-free facilities such as indoor ramps.	Building Electrical
Broadcast and television systems	1.Interior ceiling design and speaker arrangement 2.Determination of the arrangement of indoor closed-circuit television and various information broadcasting systems (hanging, hanging, leaning against the wall or independently placed).	electric
Logo advertising system	1.The shape and arrangement of signs or sign light boxes in the indoor space. 2.The modeling and arrangement of advertisements or advertising light boxes and advertising objects in the indoor space.	Building Electrical
Furnishing art system	1.Determination of the use of furniture, carpet function configuration, modeling, style and style. 2.Determination of the variety of indoor greening configuration methods, daily management methods. 3.Interior special sound effects, odor effects, etc. 4.Selection and layout of interior environmental artworks (paintings, wall decorations, sculptures, photography and other works of art). 5.The configuration of other indoor objects (public telephone covers, dirt cones, smoking sets, tea sets, etc.).	Relatively independent,the interior design major can independently conceive or select artworks, and commission artists to create supporting works

6.2 Construction of Living Spaces Design

Implementation Procedure of Living Spaces Design

In the realm of living spaces design, the implementation phase signifies the project's shift into construction. At this juncture, the design blueprints transition from the drawing board to the hands of the construction team. Yet, a designer's job doesn't wrap up with the handoff. The design's triumph hinges on a tight-knit dance with the build crew, ironing out any kinks that the real-world throws at the original vision, and sweating the small stuff to make sure everything comes together without a hitch.

As the hammers swing and saws buzz, designers might hit snags when cost-cutting suggestions come into play—be it swapping materials, tweaking techniques, or skimping on quality. Standing guard over the design's soul is part of the gig, making sure the end result doesn't stray from the dream. Nailing down the nitty-gritty of the construction documents before breaking ground is key to dodging bullets later on.

A design crosses the finish line only after it stands up to the test of real-life use and earns a nod from those who live with it day in and day out. For a designer, it's the whole shebang—from a spark of an idea to the final brick—that puts their talent on display and polishes their craft.

Construction Process of Living Spaces Design

Protection Work

Before the interior construction kicks off, the crew must roll out the red carpet for anything that's not getting a makeover or is on the back burner. This usually means wrapping up the front door, big windows, and the utility essentials like the water and electricity meters, internet cables, and the gas line's grand entrance. In neighborhoods where sticky fingers might be a problem, any high-value items that are just waiting in the wings need a security detail.

Demolition and Alteration Work

When it comes to residential interior makeovers, knocking down and building up walls is often the first order of business. Designers love to shuffle the deck of existing spaces to suit their clients' lifestyles. But before swinging the wrecking ball, it's crucial to give load-bearing walls and columns the VIP treatment, as they're the backbone of the building's safety. And let's not forget, structural changes shouldn't just be for show—they can be a can of worms. Other boxes to tick include cutting the water and power if needed, keeping the peace with the neighbors, sticking to the demolition script from the blueprints, and giving gas lines, exhaust vents, and AC ducts the once-over.

Fig 6.1:Scene from the phase of wall demolition work

Hydropower Engineering

Hydropower projects, the unsung heroes of construction, usually get the ball rolling. Once these pipelines are laid, they're tucked away behind

Chapter 6: Implementation and Construction Procedures of Living Spaces Design

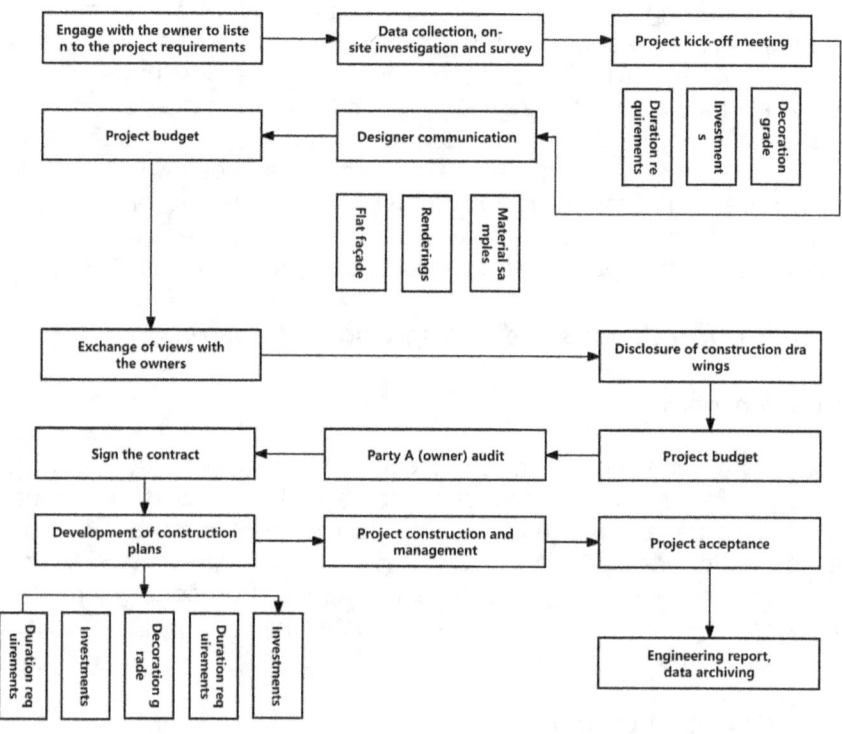

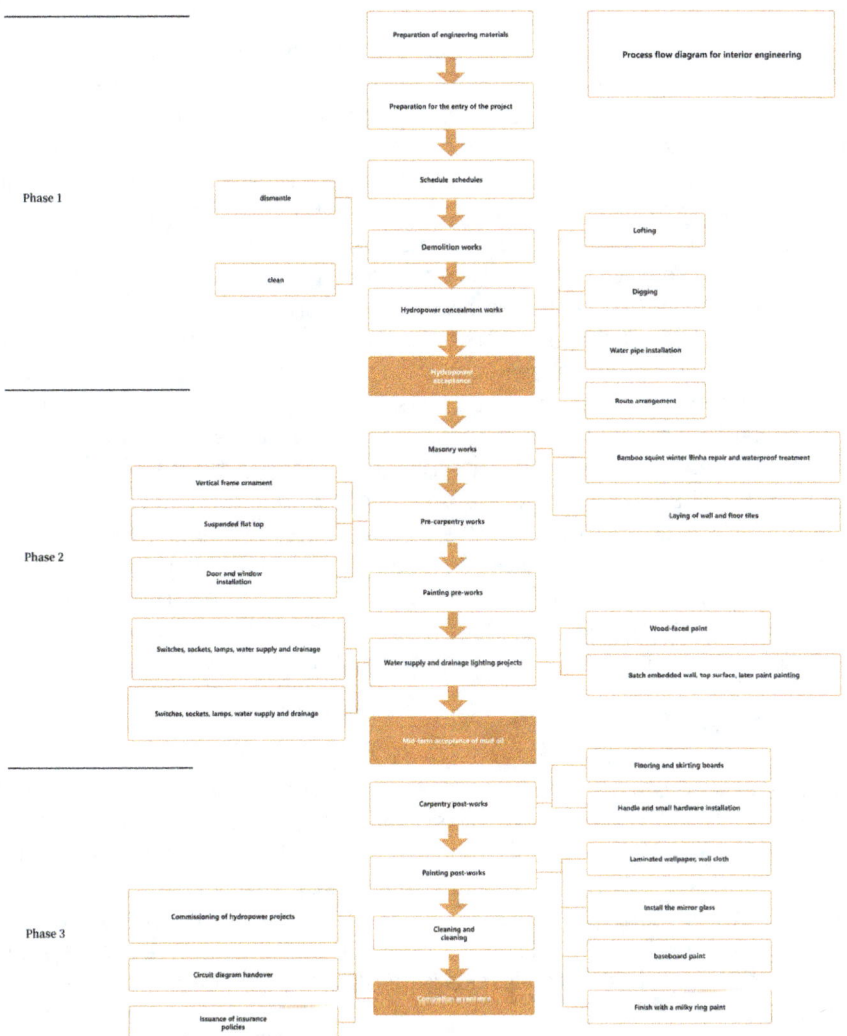

Diagram of the construction process

Fig 6.2:Top water and electricity pipes

ceilings, walls, and floors. But this is also where some builders might try to pinch pennies. These projects often dance with the masonry crew, and if circuits need to cut into the floor, it's all about syncing up with the tile team. Designers should also scout out the best spots for water meters and make sure the taps, sinks, and basins are in the right place, especially in high-traffic areas like kitchens and bathrooms. And don't forget to check the drainage slope and give the water pressure a test drive to sniff out any leaks.

Masonry Works

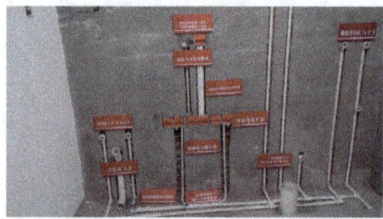

Fig 6.3:Groove the wall water supply and drainage

As the hydropower work wraps up, the masonry team is already in the mix. They're the ones laying the groundwork—literally—with new walls, floor and wall tiles, and giving the walls a fresh coat of plaster and paint. Waterproofing the roof is also on their to-do list. They've got their eye on the ball with leveling and alignment tools to keep everything straight and true. If you're using the same tiles for floors and walls, it's smart to map out the tile layout to keep the seams in sync. Smooth walls are key to avoiding cracks and other headaches when it's time to dress them up with tiles. They mix up a batch of cement mortar for the walls and floors, and after a first pass at leveling, they go in with a fine putty for round two. The painters then take the reins with latex paint or other finishes, aiming for a "rough base, smooth finish," and making sure the cement plaster fills every nook and cranny in the brickwork.

Fig 6.4:A master who is laying out the stones

Once the walls pass the waterproofing test, it's time to lay down the floor and wall tiles. This is where you've got to nail the measurements for any built-in wooden furniture, like countertops, to make sure everything lines up for the furniture parade that follows. After the tiles or stone are set, they need a shield to keep them safe from the construction stampede. And for the grout-happy spots like bathrooms, kitchens, and feature walls, slap on some non-adhesive tape to keep them pristine.

Carpentry Works

Fig 6.5:The finished surface effect of stone paving

Carpentry plays a pivotal role in interior construction, typically following the completion of masonry and the drying of plaster. This phase includes the installation of standalone wooden furniture, room dividers, ceiling fixtures, fixed cabinets, and doors. Skilled workers meticulously adhere to design plans and pre-calculate wood specifications. Each area's carpentry needs are tailored to specific spatial requirements, with detailed construction procedures established accordingly.

Fig 6.6:A master carpenter is making a wooden

On-site, carpenters can customize furniture based on design drawings and site conditions. Key pieces like kitchen countertops, TV cabinets, wardrobes, and closets must precisely match spatial dimensions during the frame production. Traditionally, carpenters crafted solid wood furniture on-site using joinery techniques, but today, fewer craftsmen possess these skills, and more furniture is sourced from specialized manufacturers. When selecting wood panels, prioritizing low-formaldehyde materials is crucial for safety, as excessive formaldehyde can be harmful. For ceiling beams, using fire-resistant and corrosion-resistant materials ensures durability. Homeowners choosing and eco-friendly materials, with suppliers handling wood measurements. In carpentry works, coordination with electrical equipment and pipelines is also essential.

Paint Works

In interior construction, wall painting with latex paint is a significant part of the painting process, typically following carpentry works. Opting for high-grade environmentally friendly latex paint is crucial due to the potential release of toxic gases from formaldehyde in chemical adhesives. Respiratory protection is recommended during application. Keeping a record of color codes for mixed latex paints is wise for future maintenance. If choosing wallpaper, the preparation involves only the wall base for application.

Beyond walls, wooden furniture crafted by carpenters often requires protective painting. Unlike latex paint, wood varnish involves multiple stages of sanding, polishing, and the application of primer and topcoat, requiring specific drying times. Note that wood varnish contains more formaldehyde than latex paint. Many interior designers now recommend using wood wax oil for finishing solid wood, significantly enhancing indoor environmental hygiene. However, most households prefer purchasing ready-made furniture. Looking ahead, modular construction methods like prefabricated interior systems may replace traditional wall construction, offering customized production and installation in one seamless process.

Kitchen and bathroom engineering

When it comes to the heart and spa of the home – the kitchen and bathroom – meticulous planning is non-negotiable. These compact powerhouses juggle the essentials: water, electricity, gas, and the unsung hero – waterproofing.

In the kitchen, it's all about creating a space that can handle the heat and keep the chef's cool. This means treating surfaces to resist splashes and spills, installing cabinets that are as stylish as they are sturdy, and routing gas and water lines like well-choreographed dance moves. With kitchens expanding their footprint in modern homes, they're not just for cooking anymore. We're talking about full-service culinary stations ready for everything from water purifiers to smart fridges. Planning electrical outlets is like playing a game of Tetris – each appliance needs its spot, with a few power-ups (outlets) in reserve. Switched-up outlet panels? A simple flick for safety and convenience.

Smart tech is setting the stage for kitchens where dinner practically cooks itself, turning cooking from chore to choice for foodies and busy bees alike. In the future, who knows? Your kitchen might just be your new personal chef.

Bathrooms, those personal retreats, demand finesse – from the vanity top to the last tile. It's all about the details: non-slip floors for safety's sake, especially for our silver-haired friends, and savvy ventilation systems to whisk away the steam and whispers of yesterday's fish fry. Dividing the wet from the dry keeps chaos at bay and makes for a serene space to scrub-a-dub-dub. As for waterproofing, it's the unsung guardian

Fig 6.7:Carpentry is working on the interior ceiling

Fig 6.8:Carpenters are working on the complex decorative ceiling

Fig 6.9:Furniture painting is underway

Fig 6.10:The kitchen space is installed to complete the effec

Installation works

The installation phase is a pivotal moment in interior construction, where various functional and decorative elements come together, including glass, hardware, flooring, and air conditioning.

Glass Installation:

Glass is a versatile material that enhances any space, whether it's used for doors, windows, mirrors, or partitions. In smaller floor plans, glass doors and windows can create an illusion of spaciousness, making rooms feel larger and more open.

Hardware Installation:

Hardware is the unsung hero of interior design, with a wide array of fixtures that serve both practical and aesthetic purposes. In the kitchen, hardware includes essentials like sinks, faucets, floor drains, door catches, locks, switch panels, power outlets, and angle valves. Bathrooms require hardware such as shelves, hooks, towel bars, toilet paper holders, soap holders, bathtub faucets, door locks, showerheads, and basin faucets. Living rooms and bedrooms also have their hardware needs, including curtain tracks, door locks, TV sockets, and air conditioning sockets. It's crucial that hardware specifications align perfectly with the carpentry details to ensure a seamless finish.

Flooring Installation:

Before laying down the flooring, it's essential to ensure the ground is level, which should be checked during the plastering stage. The area must be thoroughly cleaned without using water to maintain a dry surface. Applying insecticides and moisture-absorbing powder is a smart move, as is meticulously managing and recording the pipeline and floor joists for future maintenance.

Fig 6.11: Floor installation

Air Conditioning Installation:

Central air conditioning installation involves a complex network of outdoor units, indoor units, refrigerant pipes, drainage pipes, and signal lines. It's wise to coordinate this installation with plumbing and electrical works for convenience. During installation, pay close attention to the ceiling space dimensions, and ensure the drainage pipe is directed outdoors for easy maintenance. After suspending the indoor unit, cover it with plastic film to keep out dust and odors. A critical safety note: never install the air conditioner's outdoor unit near an outdoor gas water heater. Operating them simultaneously could draw harmful gases from the heater into the air conditioner, distributing them throughout the rooms and potentially leading to serious health risks.

By mastering these installation techniques, interior construction can transform a house into a home, blending functionality with aesthetic appeal to create a space that's both comfortable and captivating.

Fig 6.12: Installation of door sleeve wires

Soft decoration engineering

Over the past decade, soft furnishing design and engineering have blossomed into a thriving industry, adding a unique flair to living spaces design. The concept of "light decoration, heavy furnishing" has gained traction, yet many still find soft furnishings a mystery. These elements include movable and replaceable decor, excluding fixed features like flooring, ceilings, walls, windows, and architectural structures. Think curtains, sofas, wall hangings, carpets, bedding, lighting fixtures, glassware, and an array of decorative trinkets.

Fig 6.13:Expression of the effect of the restaurant

Soft furnishing engineering is akin to dressing a space—it prioritizes aesthetics, layering, and rhythm over the rigidity of hard living spaces design. Artistic flair heavily influences a designer's vision. A soft furnishing designer must not only possess a keen eye for beauty and cultural sophistication but also wear multiple hats: 1) a salesperson adept at gleaning customer insights and negotiating with clients; 2) a creative mind who interprets styles and crafts design proposals; 3) a meticulous quality inspector overseeing procurement, product quality, and project timelines; and 4) a diligent project manager handling on-site logistics and post-sale support.

Fig 6.14:Expression of the Kitchen Design

The realm of soft furnishing engineering encompasses a diverse array of products, from furniture and lighting fixtures to carpets, curtains, decorative paintings, floral arrangements, decorative items, greenery, and even tableware. Designers tailor the interior space to the owner's tastes and preferences. Once the soft furnishing design is set, procurement and installation follow suit. This design process takes into account the interior's spatial dimensions, the owner's lifestyle, interests, and financial considerations. It meticulously plans a soft furnishing scheme that mirrors the homeowner's vision and personal style, ensuring a one-of-a-kind ambiance. Unlike the permanence of hard interior engineering, soft furnishings offer the flexibility to be swapped out and refreshed to suit the owner's evolving needs, infusing the home with new life and character.

Fig 6.15:Expression of the scheme effect of the soft decoration design of the study

Fig 6.16:Expression of the scheme effect of the soft decoration design of the leisure balcony

Fig 6.17:Soft decoration scene with the theme of tie-dyeing process

Acknowledgements

This book marks the first professional English publication by myself and my team, released outside of China. Within its pages, we extensively employ design cases and methodologies from within China, with the aim of presenting the unique design perspectives and aesthetic concepts of Chinese authors to a global audience. The journey of crafting this book was fraught with challenges, including the integration and organization of content, the creation of visual works, and the adaptation to English book writing standards.

I am deeply grateful to my wife, Dr. Chen Xi, for her unwavering support of my design career and research endeavors, and for dedicating considerable time and energy to the completion of this book. My esteemed colleague, Professor Huang Yan, who is one of the authors, has made significant contributions to the theoretical aspects of the book. My student, Wang Jin, also an author, provided a wealth of materials, meticulously proofread the manuscript, offered invaluable feedback on its writing, and designed the book's cover. My student, Wang Shiyu, undertook the layout design and text proofreading for this book. Additionally, we wish to extend our heartfelt thanks to Zou Lingqi, Su Hailu, Xu Weiwen, Zhang Yuhan, Pan Yinjun, Lu Jiaqi, Xu Xiaoxian, Yao Jiazheng, and He Jing for their efforts and assistance. We are also indebted to JAN, the Asian Culture Publishing House in the United States, and the diligent and patient guidance of editor C, whose efficient work was instrumental in the successful completion of this book.

Concurrently, the writing of this book has been generously supported by funding from the following institutions:

1. China Ministry of Education Industry Education Collaborative Education Project (231003221251846)
2. Zhejiang University of Technology Graduate Education Achievement Project (2023317)

Copyright Information Table

Image ID	Description	Copyright Holder	License Type
Fig 1.1	Designed	Huang Yan	Original
Fig 1.2	Designed	Huang Yan	Original
Fig 1.3	Designed	Yao Jiazheng	Original
Fig 1.4	Designed	Huang Yan	Original
Fig 1.5	Photographed	Jasmine	Original
Fig 1.6	Photographed	Hari	Original
Fig 1.7	Photographed	Huang Yan	Original
Fig 1.8	Photographed	Huang Yan	Original
Fig 1.9	Designed	Huang Yan	Original
Fig 1.10	Designed	Zou Lingqi	Original
Fig 1.11	Designed	Huang Yan	Original
Fig 1.12	Designed	Zou Lingqi	Original
Fig 1.13	Designed	Huang Yan	Original
Fig 1.14	Designed	Zou Lingqi	Original
Image ID	**Description**	**Copyright Holder**	**License Type**
Fig 2.1	Designed	Zou Lingqi	Original
Fig 2.2	Designed	Xu Xiaoxian	Original
Fig 2.3	Hand-drawn	Pan Yijun	Original
Fig 2.4	Designed	Xu Xiaoxian	Original
Fig 2.5	Designed	Xu Xiaoxian	Original
Fig 2.6	Hand-drawn	Pan Yijun	Original
Fig 2.7	Designed	Zou Lingqi	Original
Fig 2.8	Designed	Pan Yijun	Original
Fig 2.9	Designed	Pan Yijun	Original
Fig 2.10	Designed	Zou Lingqi	Original
Fig 2.11	Designed	Pan Yijun	Original
Fig 2.12	Designed	Pan Yijun	Original
Fig 2.13	Designed	Pan Yijun	Original
Fig 2.14	Designed	Zou Lingqi	Original
Fig 2.15	Designed	Pan Yijun	Original
Fig 2.16	Designed	Xu Xiaoxian	Original
Fig 2.17	Designed	Pan Yijun	Original
Fig 2.18	Designed	Pan Yijun	Original
Fig 2.19	Designed	Pan Yijun	Original
Fig 2.20	Designed	Pan Yijun	Original
Fig 2.21	Designed	Zou Lingqi	Original
Fig 2.22	Designed	Pan Yijun	Original
Fig 2.23	Designed	Xu Xiaoxian	Original
Fig 2.24	Designed	Pan Yijun	Original
Fig 2.25	Designed	Pan Yijun	Original
Fig 2.26	Designed	Pan Yijun	Original
Fig 2.27	Designed	Pan Yijun	Original
Fig 2.28	Designed	Pan Yijun	Original

Image ID	Description	Copyright Holder	License Type
Fig 2.29	Designed	Pan Yijun	Original
Fig 2.30	Designed	Xu Xiaoxian	Original
Fig 2.31	Designed	Pan Yijun	Original
Fig 2.32	Designed	Pan Yijun	Original
Fig 2.33	Designed	Pan Yijun	Original
Fig 2.34	Designed	Zou Lingqi	Original
Fig 2.35	Designed	Zou Lingqi	Original
Image ID	**Description**	**Copyright Holder**	**License Type**
Fig 3.1	Designed	Lu Jiaqi	Original
Fig 3.2	Designed	Lu Jiaqi	Original
Fig 3.3	Designed	Xu Weiwen	Original
Fig 3.4	Designed	Xu Weiwen	Original
Fig 3.5	Designed	Lu Jiaqi	Original
Fig 3.6	Designed	Lu Jiaqi	Original
Fig 3.7	Designed	Lu Jiaqi	Original
Fig 3.8	Designed	Lu Jiaqi	Original
Fig 3.9	Designed	Xu Weiwen	Original
Fig 3.10	Designed	Xu Weiwen	Original
Fig 3.11	Designed	Lu Jiaqi	Original
Fig 3.12	Designed	Xu Xiaoxian	Original
Fig 3.13	Designed	Xu Xiaoxian	Original
Fig 3.14	Designed	Xu Xiaoxian	Original
Fig 3.15	Designed	Lu Jiaqi	Original
Fig 3.16	Designed	Xu Xiaoxian	Original
Fig 3.17	Designed	Xu Xiaoxian	Original
Fig 3.18	Designed	Xu Weiwen	Original
Fig 3.19	Designed	Lu Jiaqi	Original
Fig 3.20	Designed	He Jing	Original
Fig 3.21	Designed	Lu Jiaqi	Original
Fig 3.22	Designed	He Jing	Original
Fig 3.23	Designed	He Jing	Original
Fig 3.24	Designed	He Jing	Original
Fig 3.25	Designed	Xu Weiwen	Original
Fig 3.26	Designed	He Jing	Original
Fig 3.27	Designed	Lu Jiaqi	Original
Fig 3.28	Designed	He Jing	Original
Fig 3.29	Designed	Lu Jiaqi	Original
Image ID	**Description**	**Copyright Holder**	**License Type**
Fig 4.1	Designed	Zhang Yuhan	Original
Fig 4.2	Designed	He Jing	Original
Fig 4.3	Designed	Yao Jiazheng	Original
Fig 4.4	Designed	Zhang Yuhan	Original
Fig 4.5	Designed	Yao Jiazheng	Original
Fig 4.6	Designed	Zhang Yuhan	Original

Image ID	Description	Copyright Holder	License Type
Fig 4.7	Designed	He Jing	Original
Fig 4.8	Designed	Zou Lingqi	Original
Fig 4.9	Designed	Zou Lingqi	Original
Fig 4.10	Designed	Zou Lingqi	Original
Fig 4.11	Designed	Zou Lingqi	Original
Fig 4.12	Designed	Zhang Yuhan	Original
Fig 4.13	Designed	Zou Lingqi	Original
Fig 4.14	Designed	Zou Lingqi	Original
Fig 4.15	Designed	Yao Jiazheng	Original
Fig 4.16	Designed	He Jing	Original
Fig 4.17	Designed	Zhang Yuhan	Original
Fig 4.18	Designed	Xu Xiaoxian	Original
Fig 4.19	Designed	Xu Xiaoxian	Original
Fig 4.20	Designed	He Jing	Original
Fig 4.21	Designed	Xu Xiaoxian	Original
Fig 4.22	Designed	Xu Xiaoxian	Original
Image ID	**Description**	**Copyright Holder**	**License Type**
Fig 5.1	Hand-drawn	Wang Jin	Original
Fig 5.2	Hand-drawn	Wang Jin	Original
Fig 5.3	Hand-drawn	Wang Jin	Original
Fig 5.4	Hand-drawn	Wang Jin	Original
Fig 5.5	Designed	Yao Jiazheng	Original
Fig 5.6	Designed	Yao Jiazheng	Original
Fig 5.7	Designed	Yao Jiazheng	Original
Image ID	**Description**	**Copyright Holder**	**License Type**
Fig 6.1	Designed	He Jing	Original
Fig 6.2	Photographed	Jin Yang	Original
Fig 6.3	Photographed	Jin Yang	Original
Fig 6.4	Photographed	Jin Yang	Original
Fig 6.5	Photographed	Jin Yang	Original
Fig 6.6	Photographed	Jin Yang	Original
Fig 6.7	Photographed	Jin Yang	Original
Fig 6.8	Photographed	Jin Yang	Original
Fig 6.9	Photographed	Jin Yang	Original
Fig 6.10	Designed	Su Hailu	Original
Fig 6.11	Photographed	Jin Yang	Original
Fig 6.12	Photographed	Jin Yang	Original
Fig 6.13	Designed	Su Hailu	Original
Fig 6.14	Designed	Su Hailu	Original
Fig 6.15	Designed	Su Hailu	Original
Fig 6.16	Designed	Su Hailu	Original
Fig 6.17	Photographed	Jin Yang	Original

www.ingramcontent.com/pod-product-compliance
Lightning Source LLC
Chambersburg PA
CBHW051213290426
44109CB00021B/2437